# STRANGE S

# of a

# WW2 RAF

# NAVIGATOR

## Peter Arton

## (Salo Apfelbaum)

# PROLOGUE

Passover 1954. Another name for the Jewish festival is *The Season of our Freedom.*

Jews all over the world sit together with family and friends over a festive meal and read the *Hagada* – which tells the story of the Jews' exodus from Egypt.

Sitting in solitary confinement in a cell in London's notorious Brixton prison, wasn't exactly my idea of freedom. How did I come to be there? My first *visit* to the prison had been in January 1942, when Henry and I were interned as *foreign aliens* on arriving in England after a three and a half year journey to escape the Nazis, which had taken us from our native country, Czechoslovakia through Eastern Europe, Asia, the Far East, South Africa and finally to England.

There is no doubt that the great shock to the lives of my generation was the outbreak of the Second World War. It brought an end to our carefree youth.

Although I was a young lad of only eleven when Hitler rose to power in neighbouring Germany, we children were very aware of the ramifications. The Czechs could not understand how none of the great democracies protested when they saw Germany depriving fundamental human rights to a sector of its own population, the Jews.

As the Nazis penetrated Czechoslovakia, our parents made plans to leave the country. However, events moved faster than bureaucracy, and when the war broke out in September 1939, my father and sister were already safely in England. My brother, Henry, my mother and myself were stuck in Europe. By some amazingly fortuitous circumstances, Henry and I managed to reach England, where we joined a Czech squadron of the RAF.

After the war, I returned to Czechoslovakia full of intentions to help my country establish a new *socialism*. It was not long before my idealism was shattered, when Czechoslovakia started going *the Russian way*, not to my liking. I decided to get out and join my family in England.

I continued to be very active in pro-Czechoslovak affairs. My activities gradually faded till the Slánsky affair brought them to a complete halt.

Yet just a few weeks before, I had been preparing for my wedding to Claudia. Early one morning there was the dreaded knock on the door…

# Chap 1 :Czech Childhood.

I was born in Warsaw 1922. Age three, mother and we three children moved to Teplice to join father. Teplice, or then Teplitz-Schönau, a north Bohemian town near the Czech–German border. The area, then called *Sudeten Country*. (Sudety – Sudetenland)

Our language was German. Not the dialect of our nearby German neighbours in Sachsen but a more sophisticated tongue more native to Vienna. Our greeting was the formal *servus* as heard In Vienna, Budapest and ancient Rome.

I am a *middle* child. My brother, Henry, was 14 months older then I, and my sister Steffi, two years younger. At first we lived in nearby Proboštov, (Probstau) a one hundred per cent German village, so father could be near his business, a hand-spinning outfit. Later also manufacturing ladies' stockings. As Henry and I reached school age, we moved to Teplice.

Better schooling, social life, sports and a synagogue. Some years later father gave up hosiery as fully fashioned stockings (with a seam in the back) became the rage, requiring expensive *flat-bed* knitting machines.

The new business, now in Teplice, buying ends and faulty woven sections of woven fabrics from weaving mills in Germany, mainly in the Chemnitz area. They came in square pressed bales of 200 kg each. Father rented a huge warehouse, where rows of girls sat sorting the materials according to colour. Separated and again baled, they were sold to factories that shredded them, ultimately spun into recycled yarn. This yarn was used mainly for weaving army blankets. The Italians developed a process to make fine flannel fabrics from these yarns.

There is proof of a Jewish presence in Teplice from as far back as 1414, and records exist of a synagogue in 1550. It was probably built in 1480 and survived German occupation. It was destroyed in the fifties, during the Communist era, together with the whole Jewish Quarter. Sometime in the seventeenth century, the Jews were expelled from the town and had to live in nearby Sobědruhy (Soborten). By the late 18th century, the 430 Jews in the ghetto of Teplice and Soborten comprised one third of the population. After 1848, all restrictions for Jews were lifted and the community was entitled to the same rights as the rest of the population. By the 1920s, there were some 5000 Jews in Teplice out of a population of 35,000.

The town had many parks and it was the oldest spa. According to a monument at the original well, a hot spring was discovered when a piglet fell into it! Teplice also boasted many industrial companies: Kunert's hosiery factory, Edelstein's knitting concern and my uncle Kurländer's carton plant. My uncle moved to Palestine before world war II and manufactured cartons in Tel Aviv. He left for Europe a couple of weeks before the war broke out. Was never heard of again.

Other members of our community were Rabl, who made sweets, and Propper who made noodles. Abeles' furniture factory and quite a number of clothing factories When my father came to Israel for the first time he enquired about Rabl and Propper. Rabl continued to make sweets, and *Noodle* Propper established Osem, Israel's biggest noodle company – or pasta in today's parlance. Now a huge concern of international standing.

The centre of town boasted a cultural complex. Opera, theatres and concert hall. Part of that complex, never to forget; the *Theater Café*. The main social centre for the Jewish population especially at week-ends. Saturday afternoons and Sunday mornings saw the tables crowded with Jews, not only from Teplice but also from the surrounding areas. In one room sat many ladies, heads down, intent on their bridge game. In another, sat the chess experts, in yet another, those who liked to tax their brains by cracking the crossword puzzle in the daily paper. All around was the buzz of conversation: politics argued, business deals made, future plans discussed. In some quieter corner, budding authors pored over their latest manuscripts. And for us, the younger generation? The wide pavement outside was the *Via Veneto* of Teplice. This was where boy met girl. And after the war:

a meeting place for the few of us who were left. Some in uniform, others lucky enough to survive concentration camps.

Near the theatre, along the same street, was Donau's fashion shop and Brada's toyshop. Both families had sons the same age as Henry and I. During the war, by chance, I met the younger Donau, of all places, in a streetcar in Shanghai. I thought I would be the only European travelling with the Chinese in the cheap section of the tram. Then I spotted another European boy at the far end of the tram – he was the younger of the Donau brothers. I met him again in London in an English Navy Uniform. We met a number of times. He did not survive the war. Neither his brother nor did the Brada boys. I met father Brada in Tel Aviv in the fifties – making toys. A broken man. His daughter, much younger than the boys also lived in Tel-Aviv.

Situated high up on a hill overlooking the town and near the centre, stood an impressive church. Nearby was an imposing synagogue, which was destroyed by local Germans on the night of March 14/15, 1939. Visible from many parts of town, this was a sight I missed on my first visit in 1945, after the war. Although I had never heard of *Reform* Jews, this synagogue could hardly be called orthodox. Although men covered their heads and the women sat separately, up in the balcony, the choir, accompanied by an organ, enhanced Friday night services.    When    Rabbi Weiss gave his sermon, you could hear a pin drop. We children sat in the front rows for the Rabbi to see our presence.

Father's good friend, Mr. Kalb, ran the old 15th century synagogue in an orthodox way. Father, having studied at a Yeshiva, enjoyed going there occasionally. Both my parents came from religious families. We kids had a traditional but not orthodox upbringing. Friday night mother lit candles and father said prayers before the meal. We kept the main holidays. Father had his own way singing the *Pesah Hagada*. On Jewish holidays we did not attend school, as was the general rule in Czechoslovakia.

Mr. Kalb's younger son, Leo, was one of the members of our Maccabi sport club of which Henry and I were members. When my mother reached Laurenco Marques on a Red Cross steamer in September 1942, she couldn't speak much English, but the hostess who received her spoke German well. She turned out to be Leo's fiancé. Later, in Israel, Leo ran his own gym.

Father was a true Zionist. For one year was elected president of the Zionist Organization of Czechoslovakia. Presidents changed yearly. The Zionist youth movement, to which all we youngsters belonged, was *Blau Weiss* – also known as *Tchelet-Lavan*. During school-time we had meetings, we listened to lectures on Palestine and learnt nationalistic Hebrew songs. We all contributed *small change* to the *blue box*, a collection box for the Jewish National Fund, an item in every Jewish home worldwide in those days. We went on wonderful hikes in the beautiful Bohemian countryside. We did not need to take water with us, we could freely drink from the wonderful unpolluted fresh springs.

One could say I had my first taste of socialism when I attended a *Blau-Weiss* summer camp in North West Slovakia. On arrival we were all asked to surrender the pocket money our parents had given us, so we should all start as equals. I carefully observed what the other children gave, I gave the same, and kept the rest.

One extremely hot day, whilst out hiking we asked our leader if we could have ice cream. A torrent of political verbiage was the response. Water was quite enough! Once the leader was out of sight, I bought ice cream for my whole group. After we had indulged in the forbidden fruit, one conscientious young socialist reported this *crime* to the group leader, who asked me if I had any more hidden money. *I haven't got any more*, I lied.

The following year I attended a YMCA scout summer camp, again in North West Slovakia, somewhere in the region of Bytča. We were all dressed alike, shirt and shorts the same colour, with a knotted scarf at our necks. The camp was run with military precision, awoken at dawn by a bugle call, washing in the nearby river, making our tents ship-shape, then standing at attention in military fashion in front of the tent for inspection. With the tents built in a circle, Indian style, it was an impressive sight. There was a prize for the tidiest tent. My tent never seemed to deserve that prize.

Every day a different boy, of the older ones, was going through tests to be accepted in the rank of *Scouts.* 24 hours he was not to utter a single word. With darkness he had to go to a higher positioned place, light a fire, visible from the camp and keep the fire going all night. No sleeping. At the next day's ceremony he was awarded the real *Scout Scarf.*

I didn't like the strict discipline, nor did another Teplitzer friend. We stuck it out a couple of weeks, then the two of us, aged twelve, decided to make for home. Over 400 km away. We left camp unnoticed. Hitchhiked from car to car. Slow going to reach Bratislava. There luck was on our side. Got a lift all the way to Prague. Hearing our story, the car owner insisted that we go to his home in Prague and telephone parents. He lived in Vodičková, near the Alcron hotel. Parents must have been informed that we disappeared. They were not just worried, they were frantic. Insisted, no more hitchhiking. To take the train home.

Sport was very popular in Czechoslovakia and very competitive. The biggest sport organization was the Sokol, all Czech. Sokol had a branch in every school, even in the smallest village. Jewish sport clubs, Maccabi,

Bar Kochba were on a very high level. Sokol organized yearly huge gymnastic displays, with light athletic competitions in Prague; *Sokolský slet*. Pupils in every school practiced for the gymnastic performance, even if they were not going to participate.

Once in Teplitz we joined Maccabi. It was run by a non-Jewish German. The Czechoslovakia's best water-polo team was Bar Kochba Bratislava. The team played at a competition in London in 1938 and they all *defected,* stayed in England. One of them I met at an Army course.

Henry and I loved sports. All types of light athletics and skiing. Henry was also top in swimming. We won numerous medals. We participated in school competitions, as well as those organized by Maccabi. The light athletic and ski competitions took place at a mountain resort called Zinwald, right on the border with Germany. Maccabi teams also came from across the border, mainly Dresden and Chemnitz. As kids we crossed over to the German part of Zinwald to buy tastier chocolates. After the Nazis took over the Germans came to us to buy.

In Teplice, we lived in a suburb called Schönau. A long two storey building. Ours was on the ground floor. The street is a cull-de sac. We lived at the end of the street, Waage Strasse, now Křičková. From our house there were foot paths, leading to a park, the highest part of Schönau and down to a parallel street.

The milkman came every day in a horse drawn cart. From a huge canister he filled the milk into jugs, the housewives came out with. Milk had to be cooked. It wasn't pasteurized. Pasteurized milk in small bottles appeared in the mid-thirties. We boys used to have such fun running after the horse and cart, and people would collect the horse droppings as manure for their gardens.

It is during that time that we got our first refrigerator. Made by *Frigidaire*. Probably the first ones who made them, as that name was used for many years depicting this appliance, like *Singer* for sewing machines and *Hoover* for vacuum cleaners. It is before that time that we had the first telephone. Eight subscribers were on one line. It did not take us long to find who the other seven were. Ideal to have group telephone meetings, not to the liking of parents, who found their lines busy for hours. Father had a single line in the office, thus no-one could interfere.

We were very friendly with the Weinbaum family. Their daughter Wishia, my age. Lonjio, their son some years older. He was an excellent violinist. My first concert ever to hear, was when Lonjio played Tchaikovsky's violin concerto at the Teplitzer concert hall. I think he was 15. Father bought his record to play on our gramophone, which looked like the logo of *His Masters Voice* record company. The records were at 78 speed. Long play records at 33 speed appeared in the late forties. When I lived in London, Saturdays I started at 8am at Harrods' huge barber shop. Always the same barber, number 20. Then to the gramophone section. There I bought the first ever long play records. The only company making these was *Decca.* Harrods already had a credit card system, only valid for their shop.

Mrs Weinbaum was my piano teacher. I gave up as she would hit my fingers with a ruler when I made a mistake. Three of the Weinbaums perished in the holocaust The story I heard about Wishia, that she was the lover of an SS officer who killed her just before the end of the war.

Primary school, all German, was at the lower part of Schönau. Five years the same teacher. Coincidentally, the alphabetically first five pupils in class were Jews. Abeles, Adler, Alexander, Alfus, Apfelbaum. Abeles perished in the holocaust. Adler, Alexander and myself served in the Royal Air Force during WWII. Adler and Alexander served in English Lancaster squadrons. Alexander in a Pathfinder squadron. Both not with a Czech squadron because of their Czech language barrier. Unlike myself, after primary school they continued at a German high school. Hans Alfus was in Palestine.

When I met Hans in 1953, he was major in the Israeli Air Force as Chanan Geyor. Advanced to the rank of General. Was Military Attaché in the Far East. His last assignment, Head of Shekem.

Teplice was a lovely and lively town, they called it little Paris. Full of parks, beautiful buildings. At the eastern end the Doubravka, a small mountain. At the foot of the mountain was the elegant *Café Panorama*. On sunny Sundays, like a procession people walked up to that café. There was always some entertainment program.

Teplice had a street car. There were very few private cars. With Henry we only used the streetcar to the end station, Duby (Eichwald), to walk up to Zinwald (Cinověc), even whilst carrying skis. Took 70 to 90 minutes, depending on the weather or amount of snow. There was a bus going up, we didn't use it even once. Parents and Steffi did.

From the first grade of primary school Henry and I skied to school in winter, taking advantage of Schönau's higher position. Though German, there was virtually no anti – Semitism. Problems started in 1933 when Hitler came to power. That was also the year I was due to start high school. Henry already finished the first year at the German Commercial high school. For me parents decided I should study at a Czech Gymnasium. As Teplice had only German ones, the alternative was nearby Duchcov, a 20 minutes train ride away. The choice was the Realné Gymnasium. We spoke German at home and none of us could speak Czech but for a spatter of words picked up from Czech friends. The other problem, I was not familiar with Latin letters. At the German primary school we used Gothic only. It was  decided to use the summer holidays, before entering high school, to send me to a Czech family. The choice was a family in Zeleneč, near Prague, who in turn sent their daughter to us, to improve her German.

I arrived at their home with a minimum of Czech and that with a strong German accent. I was very well received by neighbourhood children. Being good in sports was an advantage. Enjoyed playing  football and other games with them. I became quite attached to my foster parents. Went to  church on Sundays with  them, as all the other children in my Sunday best.

Country life was a totally new experience for me. Chickens, pigs, geese, and cows were kept on the farm. The family grew their own vegetables and produced their own dairy products. I was given various daily tasks such as collecting the eggs from the chicken coop in the early morning also feeding the chickens and pigs. One of the piglets I got attached to. It followed me around, loved to be patted, I even gave it a name. I took it for walks, like a dog. Came the moment, when this piglet had to be sacrificed for a festive meal. A great village party. Singing, drinking  beer. A lot of it. I cried and ran away till the late evening.

Could also not witness how the geese were fed. A thick elongated piece of food pushed down their throat by force.

My Zeleneč *father's* profession was zvěrokleštič, castrating pigs and swine. I accompanied him on his assignments every day. My Czech mother fortified us for the day with wonderful farmhouse bread spread with a thick layer of fat (not kosher). We rode by bicycle, 20-25 km a day through the countryside to the farms. Father knew exactly where to go and when. No telephones, faxes, or e-mails! In each village, we would stop at the local, where father would drink quite a few beers. The village farmers knew where to find him. They would come to arrange a future appointment. Despite the beers, father remained slim, thanks to the cycling!

There was of course another way the farmers knew the *pig man* was in the village. Whilst operating on swine, four men would hold them down. No anaesthetic. Pigs castrating was easier they underwent this operation when still very young. The swine much older and bigger. Had to have their belly cut open then sewn together again. The squeals reverberated throughout the village. While the operation was in progress, I went as far away as possible, out of earshot, as did all the village dogs. Though they were quick to pounce on the tasty tidbits when the operation was over.

A very popular village native came every week-end. Karel Kosina was the author of paper back crime stories, based on Al Capone. We all watched as he put one big photo in front of him, based on which he typed the story with a portable typewriter at an unbelievable high speed. He devoted much of his time playing with us a trivia game. I met him after the war. He was chief editor of the Trade Union newspaper *Práce* . I had a few sessions with him. He wanted to write my war time experience. I was not very clever not to let him go on. True, it wasn't very accurate, but definitely much more interesting for the reader, than my inexperienced writing.

At summer's end, I returned home ready to start high school. I had a 20 minute walk to the railway station. Another 20-minutes at the other end. Two carriages were assigned for school children. Our most important occupation on the journey was to copy homework from each other. The French professor, a little guy with thick glasses, definitely didn't like me. It was mutual. My homework he loved to check every time and always the same remark: you must have copied it from someone in the train. He loved it when I pronounced a French word wrongly. He only did this with me.

After the war, working at the Air Force headquarters, I was called one day by a guard at the entrance of the building. *A professor of yours from Duchcov would like to talk to you.* I went down, as visitors were not admitted into the building. The professor of French is the last I would have expected. He wanted, not less, than that I should vouch for his loyalty during the war. His request alone meant that he is suspected to have collaborated with the Germans. I now understood why he did not like me.

The walk from the railway station in Duchcov led along lake Barbara. Wintertime we skated and played ice hockey on it. Two school bags on each side were the goal posts. Skates were not attached to shoes. We used our usual half high winter boots. The skates had two movable gadgets to fix to the front and back part of the shoes as tight as possible with a suitable key. Skates permanently fixed to the shoes were used by professional skaters and ice hockey players.

The transition from a German-speaking to a Czech-speaking school was not easy. I knew as much Czech as I could pick up during the two months summer holiday. I didn't know any of the pupils. Professor Jiři Majer, a classmate, in his *z hlubin vzpomínek* writes about me *in the course of one year he managed to master Czech so well, that he advanced with us to the higher class*.

True I learned the language fast, despite the fact that I spoke Czech only in the mornings, at school. Once I got home, it was German again. German at home, German with all my friends in Teplice. Summer holidays if organized by *Blau Weiss*, or by the Scout movement, all German. Cinema, theatre, the Maccabi sport's club, Zionist movement, all in German. Relgious classes in German. The rabbi preached in German.

At primary school I learned German folk songs and Schubert's lieder. We went a lot to the theatre and Opera. Most popular were the German operettas. We knew many operetta songs by heart. The song *im weißen Rößl am Wolfsgangsee* I never forgot. When on a two months drive with Sally and Nurit, through Europe in 1976, made a detour to that lake and had coffee at the Weiße Rößl.

Now it was Czech songs, also songs from Czech operas.

As the political climate was becoming more and more uneasy Jewish parents were interested to get their children out of German schools. Yet not many were prepared to let their eleven year old children undertake the daily train journey. Whereas fifty percent of the pupils in the German gymnasium and Realschule in Teplice were Jewish, there were only about a dozen Jewish students out of 800 pupils at the school in Duchcov. I had to change my wardrobe as well. My pigskin leather shorts were definitely not acceptable now. I loved them. Didn't matter how dirty they became. Had even many ink marks. Nothing doing, they were a sign of German culture.

Just eleven years old we were treated as adults. I had to get used to a different teacher or rather professor for each subject. At primary school there was only one teacher for all the subjects. One of the professors, really outstanding, Josef Dubias, taught history and geography. He made both those subjects come alive so vividly, that to this day,

I love to study them purely for pleasure. Professor Dubias perished in a concentration camp like many Czech, non-Jewish intellectuals. In the Czech countries one didn't have to be Jewish to end one's life in a concentration camp.

Something else that helped our geographical knowledge was a gimmick devised by a chocolate factory. Within the wrapper of their chocolate bar was a photo of the capital city of a country, accompanied by facts and figures about the country. There were 90 different wrappers to collect, 90 countries. Whoever collected all, was entitled to an illustrated album. This craze lasted some months, with everyone swapping their doubles and learning a lot of general geography at the same time.

There was no religious teaching in the school curriculum, but after school hours, at 1 pm, there were religion classes for all faiths once a week. Although not compulsory, it was accepted that everyone attend, except children with no denomination. I seldom attended.

Henry and I went to synagogue on Saturdays ,providing no skiing or hiking excursions had been arranged. When I came to Israel, I met my old rabbi, Rabbi Weiss, and, on consulting a battered old notebook, he exclaimed, *ah! My worst student.* No wonder, as no rabbi came to the Duchcov school, I had to go to the German *Realschule* in Teplice, in the late afternoons. Too complicated. Most of the time I just didn't attend.

With the rise of Nazism, the Germans gradually distanced themselves from us. When I think back, it was because they were afraid of the Nazi thugs. We were particularly friendly with a German family, the Reicherts, when we lived in Schönau. Their son, Theo, was in my class at primary school. They lived in a big villa at our end of the street, just two houses away. Herr Reichert was a dance teacher; most of his clients were Jewish. Suddenly the family disappeared. We assumed they had gone abroad. In 1945 when I returned to Teplice to see who had survived, I searched for them as well. I didn't find any of my German school friends in 1945. Most of them would have been soldiers at the Russian front, and not many if any survived.

There was a period when we youngsters became very abusive towards Germans. Fights broke out between groups of Czechs and Germans in the street, Henry and myself participating. Father continued working with the Germans and on one occasion on his return from a business trip, he brought a photograph of himself with the Gauleiter of Chemnitz. He was one of father's suppliers. Father was sitting in a restaurant with this Gauleiter resplendent in his SA uniform.

*Don't worry*, he told father, *this anti-Semitism is only for Hitler to get votes. It's nothing, it'll blow over.*

And that was the opinion of many Germans, even though they *joined the party* and participated in the rallies. They thought it was just a phase that would not last. They did not believe *these rowdies* could run the country for long.

One of the first changes, the influx of German Jewish refugees. One of the first to come to Teplice, Horst Kohn, opened an optician's shop. Henry purchased his first spectacles from him. Later he moved to Israel and opened a shop in Tel Aviv and Petach Tikva. Two families, called Last, father helped to settle. They reached England much before us.

Then we started hearing about people disappearing in Germany or being sent to a concentration camp at Dachau. Many of their wives received letters saying their husbands had been killed whilst trying to escape. In 1934 Hitler showed us more of his reign of terror when he had the chancellor before him, Schleicher and his wife, killed together with other political enemies. The same night *the night of the long knives* he had loyal SA leaders simply slaughtered, including the SA chief, his very close friend, who with his Brown Shirt thugs, more than anyone helped Hitler reach the top.

Nazi brutality was nothing new to us, though *the night of the long knives* went definitely a step higher. The great shock, that nothing could move the Western Democracies to stop supporting such a regime.

The life for us youngsters changed drastically with the opening of the *Strandbad*. An Olympic size swimming pool, table tennis, net ball games. The most popular; ring tennis, played on a volley ball pitch and volley ball itself. Also a site for Völker Ball, a game I saw no-where else. At a lower level on the other side of the pool, a football pitch. At the swimming pool were: two one-meter spring boards, two three-meter spring boards and a five meter one. At the end of the *Strandbad,* a two stories wooden structure, painted blue and yellow, with private changing rooms. All our crowd owned one of these. That is where we left our swimming and sport outfits. The very good outdoor restaurant was useful, to be treated by our parents. Our group was called the *Strandbad Bande.* From May till September, this is where we met daily.

The girls were Steffi's age, many of them her class mates. The boys a year or two older. The girl I liked most was Věra Müller. Friends since I was 11, she 9. At age 13 I told her mother, I am going to marry her. The mother, a beautiful woman, just smiled. To my bar mitzvah Věra gave me a very attractive emerald set with a pen, a letter opener and a seal. This is the only item I kept throughout the years to this very day. Věra was the only girl of our group to speak Czech as well as German, as her mother was Czech. She was not Jewish. Her father was. This I assume is the reason her parents made no effort to leave Europe.

In 1938, as we all left Teplitz, the Müllers went to Hradec Králové, the town, where her mother grew up. I travelled from Prague to see Věra. As it worked out, the last time. We both blushed as Věra kissed my cheek. We kept on writing to each other, when I was in Poland and later in Lithuania. In 1940 we exchanged photos. At the back of her photo she wrote:

Milému Salovy

na věčnou památku.

Tvoje Věra.

After the war whilst still in England I wrote to her and to the mayor of the town. The reply I got from the only Věra Müllerová in that town. It wasn't the Věra I knew. How I hoped her mother, would have dissociated herself from her Jewish husband to save the children. It didn't happen. Dec 9, 1942 all four, that included her younger brother, left for Terezín, Sept 6 1943 to Auschwitz and death.

Henry belonged to the older age group with different interests. He had already learned dancing at Reichert's school, he was allowed to go out after dinner, had more privileges.

Just 14 months older than I, always much more independent. Already in Pobstau, he was just 4 years old, he jumped into the artificial lake we often went to with parents and swam. I age three also wanted to swim. Had to take lessons. Henry became a very good swimmer, in free style, which had just come into fashion. Henry excelled. Noticed by the trainer, they took him to improve further and at 14 he was sent to Prague to an all-country competition for juniors till the age of 16. He reached the final four, though the youngest participant.

Only once did we, the whole family spent the summer school holiday together. Rented a hut in the Bohemian Forest in West Bohemia, on the Bavarian border. The locals were hand-cutting wooden parts for wagon wheels at an unbelievable rapid pace. Then connect them with iron bands and affix them with huge nails. Their 2 kids, our age, brought the long raw stumps on their shoulders, one at each end. They walked with them, as though there was nothing to it. Henry and I tried. A few steps and we gave up.

If my hitchhiking from Slovakia with a friend was daring, a childish feat compared to Henry's decision to hitchhike on his own to Paris and back. His aim to meet our cousin there, Henry's age. The son of father's brother.

When it came to sport, Henry and I were always together. In the summer in Zinwald during competitions, in the winter just to ski.

Skis were then made of wood. The sharp side edges wore out very quickly. A new invention, to put iron rims at both sides, the whole length of the ski. Henry was the first to get such skis. He lent them to me for a school competition, a 10km run. At the climb, the additional weight, was quite a disadvantage, but at the straight run and more so at the descent, I overtook everybody. Like with skates so with skis, we used our regular winter shoes.

With the grey clouds nearing from across the border, we understood war is coming close. Our carefree life would come to an end. It was for us a certainty that we'll split up. Where-ever the war would bring us, we would all meet again on February 2, 1942. Never thought war could last longer than that.

Never imagined such a brutal end.

## Chapter 2: Betrayal by the West

Czechoslovakia was created after WW1, consisted of the Czech countries (Bohemia, Moravia, Silesia) and Slovakia and the Carpatho Ukraine. The Slovak language is so similar to Czech that there is no problem to understand each other. In fact Prague radio announcers were Slovaks as well. Czechoslovakia even had a Slovak prime-minister. The Czech countries had a huge German minority of three and a quarter million, all along the borders with Germany and Austria. This area was highly industrialized and north-west Bohemia rich of lignite mines, big textile outfits, china and glass concerns. In Aussig a huge Union Lever concern *Schicht*. This area had many spas. The oldest is actually Teplice, though not as famous as Karlsbad and Marienbad. The Germans were, like the Czechs under Austrian rule till 1918. William L. Shirer in his book *The Rise and Fall of the Third Reich* wrote: *between 1918 and 1935 Czechoslovakia developed into the most democratic, progressive , enlightened and prosperous state in Europe. All the minorities enjoyed full diplomatic and civil rights, ran their own schools and institutions and even served as ministers in the central government.*

The Germans were definitely better off in democratic Czechoslovakia than the Germans across the border under Nazi rule. Yet a Nazi type party, led by Konrad Henlein appealed to the majority of Germans

The thirties were indeed a *Devil's decade* or as Shirer called it *Nightmare Years.* If the Great Powers, USA, England, France decided to give Hitler a free hand, public opinion was not with them. The Soviet Union, the only power to oppose Hitler's Germany, gained enormously in popularity. The strong left orientated songs by Voskovec and Werich were the most sung. Famous writers, like Bernard Shaw, Heinrich Mann sympathized with the Red empire. The allegiance of the top Heads of British Intelligence to the Soviets, stems from that period.

As in Teplitz, I only saw German films, was curious to know how my film star idols behaved during the war. Of those I remembered, only Harry Piel, a sort of James Bond character joined the SS. Was not permitted to act five years after the war. Theo Lingen, very popular comedian had a Jewish wife. Protected her throughout the dark period. Hans Moser let his Jewish wife go to Hungary. Re-united with her after the war. Paul Hörbiger, helped Jewish actors to flee. He produced the film *The Third Man.* Heinz Rühmann divorced his Jewish wife in 1938. She married a Swedish actor and went to Sweden. Rühmann married a woman, whose grandfather was Jewish. Lilian Harvey, British born, her father was German. She escaped from Germany. Willy Fritch joined the NSDAP but not active throughout the dark days. Marlene Dietrich, who left Germany and stayed in the USA all through the war, was very badly received, when she returned to Germany after the war. In my view, the worst of the artists was the conductor Feuchtwanger, who before each concert played the music of the wiliest anti-Semitic *Horst Wessel* song. No other conductor did this. He retained his job, was even invited to the USA soon after the war. There were demonstration against him, but he performed.

At first we only saw silent films. After each picture came the written text what was said. A pianist kept on playing throughout the film. The piano just below the stage in front of row one. The first talkies were very short sketches with a very badly sounding voice. Always before the real film. Yet the progress was very fast. Soon only sound films. The pianist disappeared. I liked Charley Chaplin better in silent films.

The stiff reparation payments the Allies imposed on Germany after WW1 caused the run-away inflation which in turn brought turmoil. An excellent opportunity for extreme political parties to appear. To deprive Germany of its few colonies, was another futile step. Across the border street fighting was for ever increasing in ferocity between three parties, Sozies, Nazis, Communists. In 1938 Chamberlain said something to the effect *why start a war for a country we hardly know anything about,* meaning Czechoslovakia. About tiny Serbia the British must have known even less in 1914, yet they entered the war. An opportunity to gain more colonies and destroy Germany economically.

Revenge was in the air. Any party with vengeance as its program had a chance in Germany. One didn't have to be a genius to know, just to veil the intentions with an anti-Bolshevik bait and the West will be hooked. Hitler could be as vile and cruel as he liked, kill and rob; *he will free us from the Russian bear.* Hitler had a free hand to turn the Kulturträger into a subhuman lawless society. He could count on the Western nations' support. Could re-arm freely, occupy the west side of the Rhine with complete disregard of the Versailles treaty. Even help to advertise Germany with the Olympic games in 1936. A free hand for Nazi-Germany to try their arms in Spain, though like other countries, they signed a non-intervention clause. We were aghast that Socialist France with a Jewish prime minister, in the best position to help the Spanish republic stuck to non-intervention, in collusion with the anti-socialist Chamberlain. Yet Nazi Germany and fascist Italy helped Franco with no restraint

Austria was after all a German country. Why not let Hitler have it. So was the Sudetenland of Czechoslovakia. Without Czechoslovakia's consent the West gave that part of its country to their beloved Hitler.

**On March 10, 1939** the Times and other papers came out with rosy accounts of the present position in foreign affairs.

*Never was Europe nearer to real peace. The next step would be a halt in the armament race.*

This is what Chamberlain told reporters.

**Five days later, March 15, 1939 the Nazis marched into Prague.**

Genral Franz Halder, Chief of the General Staff told Liddell Hart after the war. *Chamberlain saved Hitler*.

## Chapter 3: Escape

As the 1930s progressed, movement for Jews around Europe became difficult. Although we saw dangers threatened by Hitler, we thought England and France were strong, and if war did break out, it would be a short one. We could not believe the West would put up with a dictator like Hitler. When we saw the West was giving in, we were puzzled. The final straw was the occupation of Austria in March 1938. We felt surrounded. Immediately afterwards Hitler started making his moves towards the Sudeten country. We could see the Germans amongst us starting to strut around with lederhosen and white socks. For us, the writing was on the wall.

Father made preparations to leave Europe. After the Munich agreement in 1938, we moved to Prague at the end September of that year. People were applying for visas to any country that would have them. Father decided Bolivia is the easiest, but this too, took a long time. Anyway there wasn't any immediate urgency .

Parents rented an apartment in a nice area of Prague, Vinohrady, in Francouska 22, brought some furniture and many of the important items from Teplice. No particular hurry. The day we arrived, a huge demonstration on Václavské Náměsti. The whole of Prague must have been there. Never saw such a mass of people. Henry and I participated. The demand was not to give in to the

Munich decision, mobilize and fight. Ugly remarks about Beneš's flight.

The crowd of hundreds of thousands cried for general Sirový, for Military Dictatorship and fight the Germans. The call-up came, even policemen were called up. A call for young men below military age to volunteer to replace the police. With Henry we wanted to register. Yet the number of volunteers was so immense, before we even came near the conscription officer, the number required was met.

This is the end of September, we hadn't registered to any school. Father's decision to send Henry and me to an all-day English school, run by the British Institute. After seven months, when we left Prague and Czechoslovakia altogether, our English was pretty good.

Apart from that short episode when I came hitchhiking from Slovakia, I had never been to Prague. Never seen so many people in the streets. On Václavské Náměsti, Na Přikopě, Na Můstku, Jindřišská, Národní Třída, to name just a few, on all a constant stream of people. Coffee houses were packed. And then the just new cinema *Broadway*. How beautiful, the leather seats. I was so impressed that throughout the years all over the world, I thought no cinema can compare in size and elegance with *Broadway*. Saw the first American movie the *Donkey Serenade*. In Teplitz only German films. A few Czech films I saw with the class in Duchcov.

Traffic lights, big restaurants, huge shops. The elegant theatre near us, on Vinohradské Náměstí. Everyone spoke Czech ! With Henry I crossed many Vltava bridges just for the sensation of crossing a bridge. Many of our friends from Teplitz were here. Edgar Semmel, Eddy Kletter, the brothers Bondy. We never knew the Bondys were USA nationals and had no problem leaving Europe. They all went to Palestine. I visited Theo at his Kibbutz Degania Bet, near the lake Kinnereth. Edgar, his cousin member of Kibbutz Sassa, near the Lebanese border. Also Lydia, the girl from Novy Sad, who had been just a short time in Teplitz was in Prague. I met her again in Krakow. She lived there with her parents in a very nice villa. The three Bondy boys, Henry and I participated in a Maccabi light athletic competition. The five of us took many first places to the ooh of the numerous Prague team. We excelled in the short distance runs, the high and long jumps. I was first in the 400m run. Our outfits: shirt, shorts, just regular shoes. Today's sport outfits did not exist yet.

The canary I brought with me from Teplitz died. Did I neglect him ? Was he lonely, I didn't give him as much attention as back home ? This canary, beautifully, all yellow sat one afternoon on my window sill back in Teplitz. I whistled and he flew in. I didn't close the window, perhaps he would like to return to his home. He stayed. Perhaps he is hungry, how can I feed him ? I went out and bought a bird's cage and seeds I was told such birds like. Back home, I put  the seeds in one of the 2 small glass vessels that came with the cage and filled water in the second. How eagerly he ate and drank. Must have been without food and drink for quite some time. Then he sat on the wooden bar in the cage and sang. I named him zlatouš. I played a lot with him. First I teased him by putting a finger through the bars of his cage and withdrawing it again. He soon understood the game and flew to prick my finger. It didn't take many days, that he came to sit on my finger after I let him out of the cage. Soon, the first thing I did in the morning, as I got up, was to let him out of the cage. He happily flew around, sat down and sang. Eventually came to sit on my shoulder, then on the edge of my cup of milk and joined me drinking. As I started to put on my socks, he pricked me between my toes as though to prevent me from getting ready to go. I had to be careful leaving the room, as he would fly after me to the open door. Asking me not to go ? We were good friends. He would obey when I opened the cage door and flew in. Back from school, I let him out again. He sat on the books I read, on the copy-books when I did my lessons. When I was away for a few days, he welcomed me with violently fluttering his small wings. Zlatouš was a good companion. One day, back from school, Zlatouš was gone, the cage door open, I must have forgotten to latch the door, so with just a push he could open it. Before eating I went to look for him. Perhaps he fell, couldn't fly back up to the first floor. I didn't believe he would purposely leave me. I spent nearly an hour looking for Zlatouš, no luck. Back home, here he was, sitting on top of the cage. In Prague Zlatouš didn't have the same freedom. In Teplitz I had my own and very big room. Here a much smaller room I shared with Heini. The cage was in the living/entrance room combined.

Though living conditions were much more cramped than in the seven rooms in Teplitz, we didn't really have the feeling of refugees. True we left many valuable and sentimentally important things behind. The clothing we left behind, we didn't miss. We got new and more elegant outfits suitable for Prague.

March 15 changed it all. That actually was the whole idea. The Sudeten area In German hands made Czechoslovakia defenceless. The West that made Czechoslovakia give up land to safe the peace were guilty of making us give up land to advance the war. For nothing the Germans got Czechoslovakia's huge military arsenal, one of the leading Arms industries in Europe. The huge Skoda works, Tatra, Zbrojovka in Brno, the Aircraft industry. The Germans changed traffic procedure within days. Everything had to be adjusted to the German rule of driving on the right side of the road. The cars, as well as the trams. No other visible great changes occurred.

Friday evening Henry brought a guest for dinner. A young SS officer. Just Friday to Oneg Shabath! We in our kippot, the SS officer with his hat, mother lighting the candles, father singing the prayers A scene that should have been filmed. The German seemed to enjoy the ceremony and mother's food. The conversation quite natural. He asked about the meaning of the ceremony. Told us about the small town he came from. He surely didn't yet understand what his uniform stands for. Nor did we.

This in no way distracted us from reality. Nothing to wait for now, we had to get out of the country. We had all the papers for Bolivia, just arrange the fare and out we go. We were not the only ones wanting to leave, it wasn't all that easy. We had no train and boat tickets. When on April 26, it was lunchtime, there was a knock at the door, Henry opened it. Both, father and I stood near by. It was too obvious how the two, not tall but stout men in black leather coats will introduce themselves. *Geheime Staat's Polizei, ist euer Vater zu Haus.* Nobody would have believed father could be our parent. He looked much younger than his 40 years, anyway just 21 years older than Henry. Henry said father will be back in the afternoon. They left. After some ten minutes Henry went down and walked at a fast pace in the direction of Vinohradské Naměstí. I watched from the window behind the curtains. The goons followed Henry. After Henry and his shadows turned to the next street, I went down with father. Father stayed at the door. I ran to the next corner. Henry had slowed his pace to make sure I can reach the street before he turns at the next corner. No, the Gestapo men didn't suspect a ruse. They kept on following Henry. I turned to father with thumbs up. Father left in the opposite direction. He held an attaché case as to a business meeting, turned the corner and caught a taxi.

We had meticulously worked out a scheme exactly for such an emergency. The only hope, nothing will go wrong. A couple of hours later the telephone rang. I picked up the telephone. A man asked in Czech, if he could speak to Mrs. Hrdilová. *There is no-one of this name here.* The caller: *Sorry, I must have made a mistake.* That was the code for us to know it was a message from father. The person on the other line was father's dentist and friend. He didn't place the call from his apartment. It meant for us to go in two days with the afternoon train to Moravska Ostrava. All was arranged for smugglers to lead us over the border to Poland. Should have father not succeeded to make arrangements that fast, the caller would have given a different name, meaning to wait till he calls again.

April 28, mother and Steffi went to the Wilson railway station by taxi. Mother holding just a small overnight bag. Henry and I, each with a schoolbag with some books, made for the station on foot. The most important things we split in our pockets. Passports and money. Father made his own way. We didn't sit together, not even in the same carriage. By the evening arrived in Moravská Ostrava, took together a taxi to the house of father's lawyer friend Dr. Max Weber. Mr. Weber had arranged for the smugglers to get us across the Polish border. He joined us in a tram ride to the end station, walked with us a few minutes to introduce us to the smugglers. As ordered, we carried nothing, except what we had in our pockets. Our bags we had left at Weber's house. Father settled the money matters with the two unknown men, who now held our fate in their hands.

The leaders informed us the walk would take more than four hours. We three kids were in good shape. Also mother was strong, the worry was father with an angina pectoris condition. We had actually argued with father to fly to London as soon as the Germans marched into Prague. Czechoslovak nationals could go to England without a visa, yet after the Munich treaty England cancelled this privilege in fear, too many Jews flood the British isles. There was one exception. Persons having previously visited England could still go without a visa. Father belonged to this happy group. He had been to England in 1935. He wouldn't hear of it, to leave us behind.

I still admire these smugglers how in total darkness, in a deep forest, no sky, no star, they knew exactly where to go. During the walk no chance to think about *what if.* Had to concentrate not to stumble over branches, stones or any other obstacle. After some four and a half hours we came to a clearing in the forest. We were in Poland. The smugglers lit cigarettes and took a deep breath and smiled. Even for them it wasn't easy going, not without danger. A lorry arrived, we jumped into the back of it. Hours of a bumpy ride, we were in Krakow.

Henry and I were the first ones to leave the truck. It was 4 am. We were guided to the second floor to a big room with a dozen men or so snoring away. Shown two empty beds, were asleep before we hit the pillow. When we woke up, we couldn't believe there were so many bugs in the whole world. The walls, the ceiling, under the pillow. I now understood the joke about a Pole being shown a mansion with a dozen rooms. The Pole: *How will they get so many bugs ?*

Father came to pick us up. He, Mother and Steffi had been more fortunate. Father had rented an apartment. Henry and I now moved there as well. Next step, we registered at the Czech Refugee Committee. Not that it meant much to the Polish authorities. We were told, not to walk in groups, not to speak Czech or German. Polish only. Police arrested refugees from time to time and send them back across the border. Not to forget, Poland was a German ally. They were loyal partners. After all, the Nazis helped them grab a piece of Czech territory!

Having literally arrived in the clothes we were wearing, we went out to buy some. I got a job on the Refugee Committee. Every week a transport left for England. Our objective was to get on one of these transports. Though I worked there, I had no idea how the lists of the lucky ones is composed. First come, first served or? One evening I was on duty at the desk when three men, who said they wanted to register as refugees, approached me. They had Polish passports. I explained that only Czech nationals, who were in danger of being sent back to Germany, could register. They offered me a bribe. I asked them to leave. A couple of weeks later I saw their names on the list for England. Though late at night I went with a friend, a co-employee, to the *Englishman* in charge, to tell him, that three Polish citizens are about to leave with the transport for England. The *Englishman*, in his pyjamas, opened the door. We apologized for the late night intrusion, but it was very urgent. The three men could still be taken off the train. We just stood in the doorway and were asked to leave. No need to have a very high I.Q. to understand. As a seventeen-year old, I was shocked that someone could make money at the expense of people in danger. This must have been one of the Field brothers.

In Krakow we saw for the first time ultra-orthodox Jews in their long kaftans and wide brimmed black hats. Also witnessed rude behaviour towards them by student hooligans (students wore uniforms), the Polish intelligentsia. We heard of 100% Jewish towns, "shtaedtls". With Henry we took the train to one of these, Tarnow, some 50,000 inhabitants. For us a very unusual sight, like in films of a century ago. At the market goods were displayed on wheelbarrows. People travelling on horse-drawn wagons. Little did we imagine we would later use just such wagons on the way to the Russian border.

Henry, not wanting to wait till we appear on the list to go to England, took the train to Gdynia with a friend, intending to get on a ship as a stowaway. They did succeed to get on a freighter but were discovered. Lucky not arrested.

Father realized, we are not getting on any list in a hurry, decided to go to England. Took advantage of the fact that he didn't need a new visa. He took Steffi with him, as she was on his passport. Once in England, he would send visas for Mother, Henry and me. Just before they left we moved to Katowice, to an apartment of a friend of Father's. The owner had left. It was a large and smart apartment in the middle of town. Katowice was altogether a much nicer, cleaner city, compared to Krakow.

The greatest luxury, the housekeeper. A young woman, possibly a couple of years older than I.

Father and Steffi left by boat from the port of Gdynia, and arrived in England on August 15, 1939. Within days of their arrival, father procured our visas and arranged to have them sent to the British consulate in Katowice. Together with our visas were precious boat tickets, for a sailing on August 27. It only needed to deposit 200 English pounds per person to get a visa. Father had thought of this before. From Prague we sent books to Mr Last in London. Henry and I were masters in pasting two pages together and in-between was one of the big white Pound Sterling bills. From the months Sept. 1938 to April 39 we must have sent a whole library. All Mr Last had to do, take the money to the appropriate authority and get us all entry visas to the UK. No, Mr Last didn't take a penny, he just didn't have the time to do us this favour.

Now it was just waiting in comfort for the sailing day. No luck. On August 23, Germany's Ribbentrop and the USSR's Molotov signed a non-aggression pact and on August 25, all sailing from the Baltic ceased. We were trapped! The only way out now was by air and that meant Warsaw. Henry hurried there with Mother to make arrangements, whilst I remained behind in Katowice. I stayed, as the Katowice address was the only one father knew.

I continued life as always. Going to a swimming pool, hang out with youngsters I had met some time ago. I now saw them daily at their club house of the Betar movement. From them I learned a lot about Jewish life in Poland and about their movement. The songs they sang I knew from Blau-Weiss. My Polish was by then pretty good. I even read Polish books. The one I remember most is the *History of the World* by Hendryk Van Loon. With a few of the boys we were out late at night, when some drunkards shouted at us some anti-Semitic slogans. The Polish boys were used to it, I wasn't. I challenged one, the loudest, hit his chin with my right followed by my left fist. His chin bleeding, my friends tore me away. Then I realized why the blood. My watch did it. The strap broke. The end of my Doxa I had since bar mitzvah. The day after, surprise, surprise. I saw my watch displayed in a show window of a watch shop. Against the advice of my friends, I went to the police. No, they didn't ask me who I am. I gave them a very good description of the watch, accompanied a policeman to the shop. No problem, I got my watch back. It was pretty daring or foolish, considering I was in Poland illegally.

Anna was an angel. Breakfast, lunch, dinner, always ready in time. We ate together. Played cards, just the two of us. She was pretty.

Since the Stalin/Hitler pact, the war came nearer. But how near, days, weeks, months ? At the Czech Refugee Office I learned that should war break out, all able-bodied men and that included me, were to assemble in the courtyard to march east. Elderly men, women and children were told to assemble near the railway station to take a train to Kielce.

Thursday night August 31, I came home much later than usual. Passing Anna's room, door wide ajar, she laid in bed uncovered, in the nude. I didn't dare.

Friday, September 1. Six in the morning. Anna woke me. How I wanted to sleep some more! Her panic brought me to get out of bed. *Listen*, she said. There was a distant rumbling. Thunder? No, these were guns. Katowice was only eight km from the German border. I dressed hurriedly, refused to have breakfast, just waited as Anna prepared me a sandwich. Little did I know that was going to be my only food until the next afternoon. I rushed first to the British consulate. Unusual for the early hour, the gate was wide open. People milled around in the courtyard. I asked an official if this is war. *Don't worry*, he said with typical British calmness, *it's only a minor skirmish.*

I continued on to the Czech Refugee office. The able-bodied men were assembled, ready to start marching. I rushed back to the British consulate. Not a soul in sight. I didn't go back to the Czechs. I decided, as long as I have money I am not going to walk. I ran to the railway station to try to get a train, to Warsaw. The Warsaw express was about to leave. The turmoil was unbelievable. Crowds of people were all pushing toward the ticket counter. A railway official shouted, *no ticket will be sold without a police permit.* How could I, being here illegally, get such a paper? What should I do? As it turned out, having missed the Warsaw express was my luck. As I found out later, this train never reached its destination. To Warsaw the train was first going north, even nearer the German border. When the train reached just the next station, Czenstochov, the town was already in German hands. The train never continued

The next train to leave Katowice was bound for Krakow, due east. About to leave some hours later. I decided to take my chances. Joined the long queue for the ticket counter. As finally my turn came I fumbled in my pockets as if I was trying to find my police permit. People in the crowd lost patience and started shouting at me to hurry up. I did not budge and the clerk did exactly what I hoped for. Pressed by the screaming crowd, he sold me a ticket. I rushed over to the platform and boarded the train.

The two-hour journey took more than 24 hours. Soon after leaving the station, I experienced my first aerial bombardment. As the planes approached, the train screeched to a halt and the shouts everyone off the train! Everybody pressed towards the exit. Realizing I won't get out this way in a hurry, I climbed out of the window. Quite a high jump, but I did it and ran away from the railway tracks. Thank goodness I was on my own. I didn't envy the people with small children or even husbands and wives who had to push their way through the regular exits. I ran as far as I could from the train, the obvious target. As the planes disappeared we all clambered on again. A few kilometres further, another air raid. And so it continued. I soon became quite adept at jumping out of train windows. Didn't even try to reach the exit. After a few hours, the train was no longer crowded. I found a seat. At night fall, slowly, the train chugged through the darkness. We kept on stopping. Often, damaged tracks had to be repaired.

I tried to get some sleep. My slumber constantly broken by frequent involuntary stops

We reached Krakow the following afternoon, The train schedule on a big board showed there was a train leaving for Warsaw at one o'clock in the morning. I knew Lydia lives in Krakow. I had visited her there, when we were still in Krakow. This was the same Lydia, originally from Novi Sad, came to Teplitz, then to Prague the same time as we did. I knew her place. Why not pay her a surprise visit. I had a very valid reason, I was starving hungry. My last meal was the sandwich Anna gave me the day before and no drink.

They had a one family house. The whole family was in a trench they had dug in their garden. They were hardly expecting a visitor that day! They greeted me warmly. Hearing my story they served me a delicious meal.

Resisting their suggestion to rest, I decided to go back to the railway station, buy my ticket for Warsaw and then return to them. Lydia's father gave me some money to buy bread for them on the way. I should have kept it, as a memento.

All the way to the station, sirens sounded, then the *all clear*. I just kept on running. Wouldn't even know how to find shelter. Soon my luck ran out. A policeman stopped me, wanting to know where I was going. He asked to see my passport, which fortunately was with mother. He was obviously suspicious. There was panic. Every foreigner was suspected to be a German spy. I was marched to the police post at the railway station. Waiting to see what they are planning to do with me, I noticed something very interesting. Apart from the exit to the street, where I had come in, there was an exit leading to the railway tracks.

This time the Luftwaffe came to my rescue! They attacked the station. All policemen ran out to the street. I ran in the opposite direction, to the tracks. Saw a goods train and crawled under. Not very clever, but at least no longer under *police protection*. The Germans were kind enough not to attack that particular train. I lay there for some time when exhaustion overtook me. When I woke up, it was already dark and no train above me. I saw a passenger train standing at a nearby platform. What luck, it was the train to Warsaw. How crowded ! I was squeezed in like a sardine. Standing, I fell asleep. As the train moved I woke up. It was 2am.

I was dozing on and off and felt the speed of the train was increasing and thought we were making good progress. Not for long. We soon stopped. Again rail repairs. So it continued all night. As dawn broke, the already familiar shouts *air aid – everyone off the train*! As I jumped on and off the train I started to study the trajectory of the bombs. What did my physics professor teach us: *an object leaving a moving matter travels in the same direction.* I could now guess where the bomb would fall. I soon became adept at bomb-dodging.

I walked from wagon to wagon, trying to get a seat. Then I saw the lucky Czechs who were privileged to go by train. *How did they get train tickets ?* I didn't have a ticket at all. I didn't want them to see me. I had a guilty conscience. After all I should have walked! That night we reached Kielce. Most people got off the train, so did the Czechs. Amongst them was Dr. Weber, his wife and daughter. The same Dr. Weber who had arranged our escape to Poland. They must have used the same escape route.

I now had the luxury of a seat. However, for every one that left, about a hundred boarded! Dead beat as I was, I offered my seat to a woman with a baby. I felt proud of myself that I had retained my human manners. I noticed none of the Poles were that polite.

The now familiar ritual started again. We progressed a few kilometres, stopped for track repairs. Again an air raid. But this one sounded closer. Women and children started screaming hysterically. I decided to repeat my window escape. Again I was so relieved I just had myself to worry about. I rushed into a nearby field and threw myself between the furrows. I glanced at my watch, six am.

I became aware that my mouth was full of earth, my face partially covered. I carefully opened one eye, cleared the dirt from my watch and saw the time was 12 noon. How was that possible? Instantly wide awake. I looked at the sky. From the position of the sun, my watch was right. Six hours had passed. Realization, I had been knocked unconscious from the blast of a bomb. I looked in the direction of the railway track. My train was still there, seemingly intact. As I ran towards it, it started moving. I ran faster and faster, desperate. What chance did I have to catch up with it ?

For the first time, I was depressed, I continued walking along the track almost willing a plane to come over and finish me off. However, self-preservation took over. I left the railway tracks and continued walking in the same direction in the shadow of large trees. No sign of another human being.

After a couple of hours I saw men working on the tracks. I hailed them and asked how near I was to the next station. They told me I couldn't possibly walk it. They had one of those manually operated trolleys, so I asked them for a lift, but they were going in the opposite direction. They were having a rest, eating sandwiches. Not having eaten for a day and a half by then, I asked them for a sandwich.

*Why don't you give us a hand first?* They gave me a shovel and I worked with them for about two hours. They went off in the opposite direction. No sandwich. My low opinion of Poles did not improve.

I continued my march. Thanks to the rail tracks I knew I was going in the right direction. After a while I became puzzled. How was it that I was walking along one of the main rail routes and not one train passed me in either direction? My conclusion frightened me. The only possible explanation, I was just ahead of the German army. The Poland behind me, no longer existed. How long would it take before the Germans catch up with me?

I walked and walked, all alone in the whole world. As dusk started to fall, I saw a stationary train in the far distance. I ran, even though sure I couldn't possibly catch up with it. But I did. It was not moving. I had caught up with my train to Warsaw. This confirmed my worst fears that I was not far from the front line. The train was half empty. I found a seat and fell asleep instantly. I knew nothing would wake me. I had already been travelling five days. Never mind the war, the ticket inspectors kept on coming. Some young Czech-speaking Poles had joined my compartment. They were from Czech Silesia. Poland, Nazi Germany's allies, grabbed that part of Czech territory with German permission. My new friends suggested I climb on the luggage rack and they covered me with their luggage, not to be noticed by the approaching conductor. It worked. The last hours with those boys was a pleasant relief from the tension of the last few days. After Radom, no more air attacks.

For the past year we had known there would be a war, and we would have to leave home. How long would such a war last? The Great War had lasted four years. This one will surely be shorter ! The Germans have no chance to drag it on longer than that.

# Chapter 4: The Socialist Paradise

We pulled into Warsaw station at 6 am on the sixth day of the war. I knew one address in Warsaw, Nalewski, 17, the home of my mother's sister and her family, the Kaffermans. I had memorized the relevant part of the street map of Warsaw, and thought I would find the address easily. What I did not take into consideration, that I left the station by a side entrance, to avoid inspectors at the regular exit. Therefore set off in the opposite direction. It did not take me long to realize that I was not in the right place. I began to feel uneasy in the deserted street. My luck, I saw a droshky, waved him to stop. He took me to the required address. We arrived at a building with several entrances and courtyards. I banged on one of the main gates for some time, till a half sleepy porter came. Led me to the Kaffermans. A young man, my first cousin who I had never seen before, came to the door. I told him who I was and asked if he knew where my mother was. He looked at me in amazement. He had heard I was missing. His older sister I knew. She stayed with us a few months in Teplitz in 1935. From us she left for Palestine.

*Do you know where my mother is?*

*Yes,* he replied, *she's with the Karmazins.*

The Karmazins were my mother's first cousins, wealthy furriers. Many years later, when I was in the Hadar district of Haifa, I spotted a shop with the name 'Karmazin'. Stopped my car in the middle of the street and ran inside:

*Are you the Karmazins from Warsaw?*

*Yes, I'm the son!*

I ran back to the car, parked and returned for a chat. It turned out this cousin also had a sister in Kibbutz Mishmar Ha'Emek. Later, by testifying about property they owned, I helped the family receive reparations.

But, we are still in Warsaw, 1939.

The Karmazins did not live in the Jewish quarter like the Kaffermans. We had a long walk till I finally presented myself at the Karmazins' door. It is hard to recall how my mother and brother received me. I never asked if they ever believed to see me again. I couldn't have let them know I had forgotten to take my *cellular phone.*

The first thing I asked for was food. Having realised the Germans were not far behind me, I urged my mother and brother to move out of Warsaw. *You are in no fit state to travel,* admonished my mother, you must rest. Little did I know we couldn't have got out any way. Some rest I got !

This was still very early in the morning. By lunchtime, the Germans started bombard Warsaw. The town was surrounded. The army was perched high in the district of

Praga on the east side of the river Visla, from where they could look down on the centre of Warsaw.

The experience was terrifying. We went to my mother's sister Saltche and tried to find shelter together. My aunt had her son and daughter with her. Another daughter had died of a brain tumour a couple of years earlier. They had all lived in Teplice. Moved to Warsaw. I don't know why. The eldest daughter, Hanna, stayed behind with us. Was like our elder sister. She was one of the leaders of *Blau Weiss*. She managed to arrange a false marriage with a friend who had the luck to possess a Palestine Certificate. Hanna reached Palestine the day the war broke out. Together with her real husband, Shmuel Navon, were founding members of kibbutz Givath Hayim.

As soon as the bombardment started, the house was hit. We had to find alternative shelter. The best place was always near the strong gateposts that framed the entrance to each of the courtyards. We also had to be sure we could escape if the building was hit. After the artillery stopped, air attacks began. A pattern established itself – air attacks during the day, artillery at night. We could not relax for a minute. A factory making preserves was hit. Bananas and tomatoes were splattered all over the street. For the first time in my life I ate bananas and tomatoes. Never liked them before. This time I even liked them dirty.

Our only goal was to survive, scavenging for food. Even a soup of potato peels tasted good! Dead horses littered the streets. People would rush out and cut lumps out of the carcass. Terrible thing to be hungry! Hunger can drive one to do anything. We could not bring ourselves to go that far.

One morning, suddenly, there was quiet. No air attacks, no artillery. Rumours raced round the city, the Polish army, accompanied by the French, are about to enter the city. We all thought the war would soon be over.

Henry and I used the lull to visit various embassies. After all, we were in possession of visas to England. Nothing doing. All senior personnel had left, and those left behind were not interested. What we did not know, there was no way to get out of Warsaw anyway.

We were still in the diplomatic section of the town when the bombardment started again. We rushed back to be with our family, the need to be together. Mother had not come with us.

One early morning a shell hit the division between the two courtyards. Henry was on one side of the rubble, the rest of us on the other. I was among a crowd of boys who started to teal at the rubble to make a hole for people to get through. It wasn't easy with our bare hands. It took time but we succeeded. Another time Harry, Henry and myself climbed up to the first floor of a building, found a bedroom and stretched out  in the sort of *don't care* mood, we'd had enough. A sudden boom threw us from the beds. That woke us alright. A shell had landed in the room next door. Had to use all our senses to find our way out through the dense dust. We found mother and aunty hysterical, convinced we'd all been killed. We escaped without a scratch.

This existence lasted three weeks until the Polish army capitulated on September 27, and the Germans entered Warsaw. German soldiers put up stalls in the street and distributed bread. The length of the queue cannot be imagined! The population of Warsaw lined up. Soldiers kept order not to let anyone jump the line. They watched with their guns at ready. Everybody obeyed but Henry and myself. *We are Germans, why should we have to queue with the Poles* we told the soldiers, *we are Volksdeutsche.* It worked! Anyway by our accent it was clear, we are Germans. The soldiers were offering us more, but we could only carry six loafs each. Still far better than a single loaf the others got.

A Pole approached the German soldier and told him there were Jews in the queue. Henry, more quick-tempered than I, hit him. The soldier next to us helped Henry and hit that Polish guy with the rifle butt. The soldiers didn't understand but we did. The other Poles in the line didn't dare say anything. They were afraid of the Germans and they were afraid of us. Henry told the soldier what that

Polish guy said to which the soldier shouted to the crowd: *so what, Jews are also hungry.* Quite sure he wouldn't dare make such a statement only a few months later.

There was no radio, no newspaper, so *rumors* was the only kind of media. This time: the Russians are coming from the East. Our aim now, to make for the Russian lines, the only way to escape from the German clutches. Number one obstacle, to get over the Vistula bridge, the way to the East. We asked mother's sister and her children, Harry, a year older than Henry and Theresa, Steffi's age, to come with us. Her answer never left my memory: *You are refugees, we have a home here* and she added *Whatever will befall the 400,000 Jews of Warsaw will be our fate too.* Aunty must have thought it will be a hard time as long as the war lasts then return to normal. As Primo Levy said there is no way to describe what the Germans did. No dictionary has words for it.

We lost no time. Dressed, as we were, in summer clothes and with one small leather suitcase we were ready to face the unknown, that very moment. Gave all the bread to aunt and kids and off we were. Nearing the bridge; shouting, screaming and pushing of a huge crowd. The problem, the Germans didn't let anyone cross the bridge. We pushed our way through the crowd to get near the soldiers. Near enough, we shouted *Volksdeutsche* plus some blah, blah. The soldiers helped us, and across we went. For the second time we learned, our German is our greatest asset. The minute we opened our mouth, the soldiers went out of their way to help us. Could we have dreamed, our escape to the Russian side would be made easy, with the compliments of the Wehrmacht !

Number one destination, less than a two hours walk, a farm owned by one of father's sisters. Mother knew the place. Aunty and uncle gave us a royal welcome. Thought we should stay with them. They were already three weeks under German occupation, nothing happened. We had other plans. To get our strength back from the three weeks ordeal in Warsaw and carry on. Our aim was England. We had lost a lot of weight, had to get some back. This place was ideal. We felt in paradise. They made bread from potatoes. Had plenty of meat, eggs, milk, vegetables. All from their farm.

Standing at the road-side one morning, Germans on motorbikes with side cars passed asking for direction. Stupidly we answered in German. Their reaction *seit ihr Juden ? Neh,* we answered and they rode off.

Henry and I started planning our route. We went by the most pessimistic assumption, that the Russians are on the other side of the Bug, 140/160 km using the nearest way. Hopefully much nearer. All we had to go on, were rumours. That this is actually the true position, we learned finally from a German officer in Wengrow.

After ten days with aunty, October 7th we worked on our final plan. We could only walk during daylight. There was a night curfew. Even if we get the opportunity to go most of the way with horse drawn wagons, we couldn't count on more than forty km a day. Our route: Stanislawow, Wegrow, Sokolow, Drohiczyn on the Bug. We needed addresses, where to stay the nights. On that score there was no problem. All neighbours were eager we should bring messages to their relations. We also took addresses to in-between places, just in case we should not be able to reach the planned destination. We decided to walk on the main roads, a better chance to get a place on a wagon. Also not try to hide from or avoid German soldiers. Our language serves as our protector.

At first, Henry and I wanted to travel alone, and then come back for Mother. We had no idea where the Russians are. All persuasion and reasoning didn't help, mother insisted to come with us. Only later we realized, how right she was. Mothers' intuition! Had she stayed behind we would have probably never seen her again. We asked mother not to take her small leather suitcase. Nothing doing. She brought it with her all the way to England.

October 8, very early in the morning, we started walking. We kept going. Quite some time before finding a wagon not too much overcrowded. For a few zlotys we got a ride on that horse-drawn contraption. Anyway, the only means of transportation. Tremendous masses of refugees going in all directions. When we couldn't get a ride, we kept on walking. It wasn't much slower, just more tiring.

In the late afternoon we reached Stanislawow, The address worked like magic. All lines of communication being closed; everyone was anxious for any snippet of information about their loved ones. So we could do a good deed and get a place to eat and sleep over. Rumours kept on confirming, where the Russians are. On the east side of the river Bug. After a good meal and relating to what happened in Warsaw, we were off for the night. Early morning, direction; Wengrow,

Far less people on the road, but much more Army movement. Soldiers on foot, truck loads with soldiers, motor bikes. No-one took notice of us. With the exception of one short ride on a wagon we reached Wengrow *per pedes.* Like everywhere else, people were very hospitable. Exhausted, we woke up as we heard the very loud scream *raus zur Arbeit.* We jumped up. Our hosts were gone. Everybody had disappeared. No doubt they were used to the early morning visitors. The three of us alone. Then what happened looked like we had lost the chance to get out of Nazi occupied Europe in a hurry, but in fact turned out to be an unimaginable stroke of luck.

Two young German soldiers stood in front of us. They were probably a year or two older than us. As they shouted *raus zur Arbeit* again, *wir sind Volksdeutsche* we answered. The tone of their voice changed. In a very friendly way one of them said *Ihr seit Sudeten Deutche*! He recognized our accent, he came from the same area. From Karlsbad. Like long lost friends asked how we got here. We used the long prepared explanation. We were in Warsaw when the war broke out. Father is in Bialostok, the Russian side of the Bug. He has no idea where we are, so we want to get to him and come back to the Reich. In the turmoil of the war, even that sounded plausible. The Karlsbader explained *you can't just walk to the border you need a permit from the local mayor.* The boys never questioned how come we were in a Jewish area, such a thing didn't exist in Karsbad. They forgot about their mission to get Poles to work. *We'll take you to the mayor, so you won't have to stand in the long queue.* Protected by two soldiers of the German Reich we walked to the office of the local municipality. Again a huge line of people, who wanted just such a permit! Could have taken the rest of the day to get near the mayor. The soldiers asked us two boys to wait whilst they accompany mother to get the vital paper. The municipality was on a big square, very wide sidewalk in front of it. A crowd of people was standing at the kerb. We pushed our way through to see what is happening. Not a pleasant sight. Soldiers had lined up old Jews with beards and kaftans in military fashion, shouted for them to march and to sing. *Lauter!* they screamed, hitting them with sticks. Just perverted harassment and humiliation. Even the anti-Semitic Poles looked on with owe. Next to us stood a German Oberleutnant, probably in the thirties. My cheeky brother turned to him *was sagen Sie dazu? "Die sind noch jung"* was his answer. We couldn't be luckier. His answer had a meaning. Taken aback by Henry's German he wanted to know what two German boys do in the Polish hinterland. Again the pre-arranged answer. He wanted to see our passports, not in an unfriendly way. We told him they are with mother. He waited with us. Mother returned, with the permit for the three of us to go to Bialostock! The permit specified how much bread and other items of food we are allowed to carry. All in Polish. Mother showed the officer our passports. He checked them thoroughly. He wasn't a child. He perfectly understood who we are. No remark from him on that score. Now fatherly. *"How the hell do you expect to get to Bialostock?" We'll walk.* Henry replied; *We have to get to Sokolow; sleep over there. Next morning to the Bug. We'll pay a Polish fisherman to take us across the river.*

*"Permit or no permit, this is a closed area. Look, said the officer, I'll take you in my jeep. Keep walking until you reach the German control post. Wait for me after you pass it. I'll take you as far as the next control post, just before Sokolov. From there you can use side roads to avoid Sokolov and proceed straight to the border, you can do it before it gets dark. If stopped by soldiers, use*

*the same story you told me. Don't show your passports. Say father has them. The quicker you are across the Bug the better."*

How is it, we never even considered it a danger for mother going to a Polish mayor, even with German soldiers. Our Jewish name, born in Poland. What if the mayor would ask the soldiers why are you helping three Jews? Unlike us, mother did not speak an accent-less German. Why then didn't we decide for Henry to accompany the two soldiers ? Could say, mother is tired from the long walk. If we, cock sure young boys, did not consider this, what about mother? Was she carried away by her sons' overconfidence? The Oberleutnant is a different story. He wanted to help, though he understood well that we are Jews.

No civilians on the road, just massive military movement of army trucks, cars and the usual motorbikes with side cars. All in one direction, to the east. And here we were, three Jews, given a lift by a German officer! After he let us off, we still had a long way to reach the river Bug. By the map we had on us, we estimated 25/30 km. It was still long before noon. We could do it. We accepted the officer's advice not to spend the night in Sokolov, avoid it, even though, after Sokolov to the river we wouldn't have where to stay. The German officer said to hurry. We took his remark very seriously. Why did he say that? It could have been just one reason, the massive army movement east, for the purpose of sealing off the border. We and German soldiers on that last stretch. We were the only civilians. It didn't seem the new border will be so peaceful! We sang German march songs, even knew by now a song of the Panzer crews. "Ob's stürmt oder schneit, ob die Sonne uns lacht ob....." Very confident. *"That little paper from the Wengrow mayor means nothing; you won't find a soldier understanding Polish anyway. Your strength is your German."* We remembered the officer's words.

It got chilly. What must we have looked like? What was important, no-one took notice of us. October 10, Henry's birthday. He turned 19. The walk took longer than we thought. By the time we reached the little village on the Bug, it was getting dark. The first Poles we met, knew well where we have to go, to the židek, the only Jew in that village. We had to ask a few times, till we found the place. A farmer directed us to a barn.

Everyone wanting to cross the river assembled in this barn. There were already a dozen people waiting. Night had fallen; we had to wait until the next day. In the barn were two Yeshiva boys. They had crossed the border from the Russian to the German side. We thought we don't hear well. We did. They were not allowed to study the Torah, was their explanation!

The past few days we had felt the weather getting colder. As we got up on October 11, the landscape had turned white. Not an advantage to  cross a border un-noticed. Mother's little suitcase came handy. It contained towels. We wrapped them round our necks for extra warmth. Our summer clothes and shoes gave us no protection. Two fishermen came to take us across the river. Mother paid them and off to the Soviet Union.

We trudged through the wet snow. Had to cross a big field. In the distance we could see two Russian soldiers in their long winter coats with guns slung over their shoulders. They soon spotted us, gesticulated for us to stop. We pretended not to see them. Eventually they caught up with us. They could not understand Czech nor the smattering of Russian that mother spoke. They took us to their commander in Drohiczyn. Not so short a walk. Our feet were soaking wet. Entered the commander's office *Dokumenty!* he shouted not very invitingly. Mother produced our passports. Seeing the Czech passports, a transformation took place. He no longer seemed hostile. Russia and Czechoslovakia had a very friendly relationship. He was intelligent enough to know about it. He couldn't do enough for us. He gave us some food and drink and ushered us into a room with a fireplace, to get dry. It took hours. Dry at last, he got for us a droshky to take us to the railway station. Looking back it is amazing how we were treated by the first Red Army officer we met. Gone was the fear that we may be returned to the other side of the border. We were safely out of Germany. Did not to see it again till after the war.

At the station we bought tickets to Bialystock. Not like on the non-functioning German side, here trains were running, even though all the tracks had to be changed to the Russian wider gauge. Mother had a banker friend in Bialystock. We paid him a visit. He found an apartment for us. He also changed our English pounds into the local currency. *This country is cut off from the rest of the world,* was his answer to mother's question how to get in touch with father. No letters nor telegrams, never mind telephone. No communication with the outside world. We had arrived on a different planet. The good news this banker gave us, Russia was about to return Wilna to the Lithuanians. His advice to go there *that's your best bet.* So, Wilna became our next goal. We would wait there until the Lithuanians took control of the city. Possibly a chance to contact England.

A big market place in Bialostock with everything possible to buy. We bought winter coats and warm Russian boots. My Doxa watch I had to hide, Russian soldiers were crazy about wrist watches. *davaj chassy* was their favourite demand. Still, they were very friendly. We met Jewish officers and Jewish soldiers who spoke some Yiddish. Easier for us to understand. The Russian soldiers had something in common with the German soldiers. **Proud and self-confident.**

The general atmosphere was happy. Soldiers formed groups, played the balalajka, danced, sang. All this on that big market square

We left Bialystock by train on October 14. In Wilno we rented an apartment and waited. Wilno, the former Lithuanian capital, grabbed by Poland after WWI was now returned to the Lithuanians. Under the Poles it became one of the most anti-Semitic towns in Poland. Now under Soviet rule, the Poles became Jew friendly. We got the first taste of Soviet economy. Nothing to be had without waiting in long queues. Not even bread could one get without standing in line. Not just minutes, hours.

No problem to find work. Henry and myself became construction workers. We liked throwing bricks from one to the other. No gloves! The Russians paid well. Paid every day for that day's work and good wages. Some days we also worked on the railway tracks.

All that ended when the Lithuanians entered the city October 28. On that very first day the Poles organized a pogrom. Henry and I went out into the street. We witnessed Polish students in their uniforms behaving like beasts. Attacked a woman with a baby in a pram. They overturned the pram and beat her up for no reason! We couldn't believe what our eyes saw. No sign of any police. The Lithuanian army was already here, so was the police. They gave the thugs a free run.

As expected, once the Lithuanians were in control, contact was re-established with the outside world. We sent a telegram to father in London. Naturally, he had been trying to find out what had happened to us. From the Red Cross he received a letter telling him that we had all perished in Warsaw.

My father had suffered from heart problems from the age 16. When our telegram arrived, he was actually in hospital, having treatment. Imagine his and Steffi's delight on hearing we were all alive and well! He now tried to find a way to get us to England via Sweden and Norway. Easier said than done. There was no organized passenger service between Norway and England, and besides the North Sea was already full of U-boats.

Communication was not the only thing to differ from Soviet rule. From day one, no more standing in line for food or anything. Milk and meat products were excellent. Both, government monopolies. I enlisted at a school where only Yiddish was spoken. Yiddish being very similar to German was not difficult to learn. The only problem, the writing was in Hebrew letters. These I sort of learned, but not really knew as I never used them. Wilno was probably the largest Yiddishist centre. Politically most of the youths in that school were tending to be to the left. Mainly Bundists. None were religious. A Viennese boy joined our class. The only one in a Jewish school to wear a kippa ! Said prayers before eating his sandwich. The local kids looked on as though they had never witnessed this before. The picture was very odd.

The Jewish Joint entered the scene. They provided a house for Czech and Slovak refugees. Eventually all Czechs and Slovaks in Wilno came to stay and live in that house. Jews and non-Jews, 105 of us. Each family got one room. We became like one big family. The Webers came with their 12 year old daughter. Another Max Weber, also from Moravska Ostrava, probably 10 years older than myself. I met him again after the war in the rank of štábní kapitán in the Czech Army. He had fought in Russia. He commanded an artillery unit. He described with pride the tremendous power of these canons. In 1948 he was deputy commander of the Czech brigade sent by the Czechoslovak government to help Israel in the war of liberation.

Back to Wilna, now Vilnius. A Mr. Lieberman from somewhere in Slovakia was with us. An elderly gentleman, Konopásek, who kept a diary. I copied him. At his advice I started by recalling events since leaving our home-town the year before. The older members of our group organized us as an independent unit; a community. Some did the shopping. The cooking was done by a Czech pilot, Tonda Kamínek. I was his assistant. I knew very little about cooking, never even saw such big cooking pots! Just did what I was told. We had artistically leaning people, organized drama groups. Lectures were given, a choir formed.

I made many friends in school, my closest, a local boy, Mackiewicz. Then were two brothers Kushnir, refugees from Warsaw. Father wrote us he met a Mr. Amdursky in London whose wife and 13 year old daughter are in Wilno. Mother's gain, got herself a friend from the local population. Very lovely lady. Winter came, we were told the harshest ever. Temperatures plunged to below minus 40 Celsius. Schools were closed. We had to get these Russian type fur hats, with ear covers. Snow must have been near a meter deep. Our house wasn't sufficiently heated. We didn't have enough blankets either. It was terrible to be constantly cold, not just cold, freezing.

With all those problems of surviving, the main one: to get out of Europe. Many schemes came up. I think the Webers were the first to succeed. They managed to get to England via Sweden and Norway. No idea why we didn't manage. We had English visas.

There was a lot of tension before the Russians attacked Finland. The general opinion, problem could have been settled peacefully. The feeling, the Russians preferred the war. The sympathy was with Finland. Pro communists were embarrassed. Communists as such did not exist openly, their leaders were in jail. Rather odd, as Russia had returned Vilnius to the Lithuanians of their own free will! The Poles grabbed it in 1922. We enjoyed the Finns giving the Russians a hard time. Russian reason to wage war: *strategic.* The Finnish border too near to Leningrad ? By March it was all over.

More tension with the Nazis entering Denmark and Norway. The British Army landing in Norway was the first sign of unpreparedness on their part. They must have slept very well whilst the Germans armed. It was discouraging. Our escape rout via Norway, gone. Then came the real war as Germany attacked neutral Holland, Belgium, Luxemburg to get to France.

Things moved too fast to apprehend. One German success after another. Very depressing. The French will stop the German onslaught at this river, than at the next one, then .......It never came. The great French army falling to pieces.

The Russians were not idle. Occupied Bessarabia and part of Bukovina whilst Germany was busy with France. In June the Russians returned to Lithuania and this time also occupied Latvia and Estonia. Strategic movements. Definitely not friendly gestures to their new ally; Germany. The moment the Russians entered Vilnius, back were the bread lines and lines for everything. That was only part of it. Our contact with father was gone again. I corresponded with my one and only pre-war girl friend from Teplice, Věra Müllerová. She sent me a photo of hers. From the few possessions I managed to keep was the Bar Mitzvah present I got from her and that photo. The most surprising letter we got was from Harry, our cousin we spent the war in Warsaw with. A photo of his in Russian uniform. Just regards, nothing about his mother and sister. Ryvka from Israel asked about Harry's mother and sister at the Red Cross. Even got an answer in our auntie's hand writing. Contact finished. We were once more on the Soviet planet, far from planet Earth.

At school. We got new teachers, emphasis on math and science subjects. We went to free concerts, free theatre shows. A drama group was formed, a choir, Russian dances. Remembering the boys joining the Nazis in Teplice were the lowest elements, rowdies, the worst in class. Not here. To join the pre-comsomol group, jatchejka, only those at top of the class. Though I considered the Czech educational system excellent, I liked the Russian system better. Mathematics not just figures. Logical thinking. Very similar to the book *Mathematics for the Million.* History and geography, not just dates, economic backgrounds.

It was Motty Mackiewicz who convinced me to accept the communist ideology. Then something happened, stayed with me ever since. I never forgot. As the Russians entered, the communist leaders were released from jail. Obvious they will take a leading part in the Lithuanian leadership. It didn't happen. They disappeared, never heard of them again. Though I embraced the correctness of the ideology, this, more than anything else, convinced me not to accept the Stalin version. I brought this up, when I played chess with a Russian General in the Trans -Siberian railway. This was a very sore subject. Very important part of the Stalin terror, no-one should be sure if the next day he can disappear in the enormous size of the Siberian wasteland. Only later I understood, the Soviet Union could develop Siberia only with slave labour. The sole alternative, economic incentives. This requires private enterprise, in an egalitarian society not possible.

Just as I was accepted for glider training, after physical and psychometric exams placed me as number 4 out of the 200 who passed, information filtered through, that it is possible to get a Japanese visa from the consulate in Kaunas. It would be a transit visa. The requirement, to have an end-destination visa. It was not just a rumour. Visas had already been issued.

Though I, at the time didn't think it was urgent to leave Russia, nevertheless, aim number one was to reach England. One problem facing most of us was that, our Czech passports had expired. There was no Czechoslovak representation in the Soviet Union. Russia recognized the German occupation! One of the more imaginative people in our group fashioned a Czech diplomatic stamp from a potato and stamped all the expired passports with a date before the outbreak of the war, from the Czech consulate in Krakow. Using another potato to fashion an end destination visa stamp for the Dutch East Indies. We were ready for the transit visa through Japan.

The story of the Japanese diplomat, Consul in Kaunas, Senpo Sugihara, is now legendary. Sugihara issued a transit visa for everybody with an end-destination visa. He decided to help Jewish refugees to get out of Europe. All the stories that Sugihara was issuing the visas against instructions, I do not buy. The Japanese authorities could have just not recognized them and not let the refugees enter Japan. Specially in cases like ours, with false passport validity extensions and false end destination visas. All very obvious crude fakes.

Already at the beginning of the Nazi regime, Japan offered to admit any number of European Jews to settle in Manchuria. Rabbi Stephen Wise, a lackey of anti-Semitic Roosevelt, who thought himself representing world Jewry, scoffed at it from his comfortable home in the USA. When the Nazis sent colonel Meisinger, *the butcher of Warsaw* to Japan with plans to exterminate every Jew, the Japanese didn't let him touch a single one of the 30,000 Jews under their jurisdiction. They did not forget Jewish financial help in their 1905 war against Russia.

In 1940/1941, by the figures I then knew, about 2,000 reached Japan. Possibly many more had visas but didn't have the money for the Russian train, or may not have received the Soviet exit visas in time.

Henry, representing the three of us decided to go to Kaunas together with others from our group, to try their luck. I sacrificed my Doxa watch to finance the trip. We were successful recipients of that life supporting visa. My school-friends, the Kushnir brothers got it as well.

We still had to acquire an exit visa from Russia. Not so easy. Why the hell would anyone want to leave the **Socialist paradise**? It took the Russians some time to give in. We applied. My transit visa arrived first. In September, valid till December. As October and November went, our fear, mother and Henry wouldn't get theirs before my exit visa expires. Lucky, ever since we left Warsaw, also this time. First week of December Mother and Henry got their exit visas. Henry was in charge. He arranged tickets through Intourist, the Soviet government-controlled tourist organization. We had to join a group, provided with an official guide all the way to Vladivostok. We left Wilna on December 25, 1940. First stop Moscow.

The entire group, accompanied by our faithful guide, stayed at the Hotel Novomoskovskaya in Moscow for a few days. The hotel was situated across the bridge from the Kremlin, affording us a magnificent view of the Soviet power-house. It was at this hotel that I first developed a taste for caviar. Red and black caviar always at the breakfast table. Henry and I took full advantage of our time in Moscow. The famous underground system had not been open very long. We soon discovered that for the price of one ticket, we could travel the whole of the underground system, as long as we don't exit. One day we travelled to many of the 225 stations, each in the style of a different country of the Soviet Union. And then we walked, walked and walked all over Moscow, in the freezing December temperatures. At one stage we were being followed. We split up and exercised a few diversionary tactics to fool our pursuer. Maybe it worked.

We boarded the trans-Siberia railway for a ten-day train journey to Vladivostok. Four people were allocated to each compartment. At night the benches became our beds, two at the top, two at the lower section. The fourth person was a Lithuanian lady. Every day, as the train raced the whole breadth of Mother Russia, we had to move our watches one hour forward. Once a day, the train stopped and changed engines. One of the stops was Birobidzhan, the Jewish autonomous region established by Stalin in 1934. We were amazed to see the station sign written in Yiddish.

The scenery never changed. Snow and again snow as far as the eye could see. After the stop in Irkutsk, the long spell along lake Baikal was a pleasant change. This is the world's deepest lake. The only unforeseen stop one night, the strong wind blew off the roof of one of the wagons. Luckily the one containing cargo, only.

Our compartments were in the cheap class. Pricewise, not cheap at all! Each day as we made our way to the dining car, had to go through the first class wagons. Army generals were playing chess and drinking to pass their time. They were always half-drunk, like British officers. The difference? The Brits liked their whisky, whereas the Russian generals' tipple was vodka in cold tea ! I watched them for a while and then struck up a conversation with a few of them. One of the Generals invited me to play a game with him. We played together for a few days until a visiting General whispered something to my General friend's ear. End of friendship.

We arrived in Vladivostok at the beginning of January 1941. I cannot begin to describe the cold. Being a port. the wind-chill factor was unbelievable. It felt like knives cutting our faces. Vladivostok was a dreary place and so was the hotel. At least it was well heated. Our group of around 200 people left Vladivostok and mainland Asia in the hold of a 1,600-ton boat. Good bye to Russia.

That tiny boat had just one lower deck, one big space that accommodated all 200 of us. Sitting in a circle along the circumference of the hold just with mats on the floor. Our two-day voyage was a nightmare. A typhoon showed us the strength of nature. Our small boat was tossed around like a matchbox; everyone vomited. We were all thrown from one side of the boat to another. And so was the luggage. Never thought we would survive the voyage.

In the middle of it all, Henry said, enough, have to get out – we were desperate for some fresh air. As we climbed the stairs to the main deck, a huge wave pushed us down again. It was then that I decided, if I survive, I would never board a boat again, and as Japan is an island, I would have to spend the rest of my life in that country. Miracles do happen. We did survive. We all survived. Our boat lasted two more trips. On the third, caught in another typhoon, it sank.

## Chapter 5: From Kobe to  Liverpool.

Soon after we docked at the port of Tsuruga, on the west coast of Japan, Japanese soldiers boarded our battered boat. We soon understood Japanese can also be nasty. One of our group tried to joke with one of the soldiers. The response was a slap in the face. No more jokes.

The contrast between disorderly and chaotic Europe and the pristine orderliness of Japan was stark. Our destination was Kobe, the only town non-Japanese could live in. Exception was Yokohama, where foreigners involved in shipping were allowed to reside.

We boarded an unbelievably sleek, modern train, which travelled at an equally unbelievable speed! Fortunately the station signs were in English, not just Japanese, so we could see where to get off. After approximately two hours, we identified our station, but by the time we had accumulated all our luggage, the train had continued its journey and was already three stations further on. We finally disembarked and returned to Kobe by the next train in the opposite direction.

Although accommodation was provided for the refugees, we, the three of us, rented our own apartment in Yamamato Dori 16/17. The place was not one of those flimsy wooden contraptions, a solid stone house. It was Henry to arrange all this, no idea how he managed it so quickly. A small kitchen, hall and two bed rooms. The bedroom I shared with Henry was so small, just enough place for a double bed. No extra space. As we opened the door, we jumped into the bed.

According to our visas, we were only supposed to stay in Japan whilst we sought passages to the Dutch East Indies. ( Now Indonesia). Yet no one said to us, *Why don't you go*, and no-one bothered us.

We again established contact with father in London. Father was bombed out in the Blitz. Steffi's school was evacuated to St.Albans. The danger of the Germans landing in England after the conquest of France, was over. At least till the following summer

By now our money had almost run out. Father managed to wire us money from England to a lawyer in Tokyo. Mother and Henry travelled to Tokyo to pick it up.

In Kobe, Henry and I attended an English college, the *Canadian Academy*, which still exists today as far as I know. Some years ago, while travelling from Milan to Monte Carlo with Moshe Alkalai, an upholstery manufacturer, I struck up a conversation with a Japanese on the way to Lyon to buy silk. He said he came from Osaka. As he left the train, he gave me his card, where I read his address as Kobe.

*But you told me you were from Osaka.*

*Everybody knows Osaka, most people haven't heard of Kobe.*

*Well, I did, I studied there, at the Canadian Academy*, I told him.

*So did I* was his answer.

The students at the Canadian Academy were children of diplomats, Russian Jews from Harbin and children from mixed marriages, half Japanese. Although Kobe was a large, modern town, the sewage system was open, only covered with stone tiles to walk on. There was so much new and strange to us. Women nursed their babies in public. Although acceptable today, that was not the case in pre-war Europe. Many streets, just one lane to be shared by cars, bicycles, rickshaws, humans. I admired the drivers zigzagging through the multitude. We did not like the idea of rickshaws: a human pulling another human. The rickshaw men had distinctive, very decorative outfits. One day we hired a rickshaw, asked the rickshaw man to sit inside and we pulled. In fact, it was not as difficult as it looked. The carriage is well balanced and pushes the driver up. One doesn't really feel the weight. We certainly attracted attention that day two western boys pulling a Japanese rickshaw man. Though to us it looked easy, we didn't run all day! I understand rickshaw men died very young. In their thirties.

Japanese trust. After having a haircut at a barber, I realized I had no money on me. The barber made no fuss, just smiled trusted me to return. Over the months I picked up a smattering of Japanese, but do not remember a word of it today. Mother cooked for us. Occasionally we went to one of those very large restaurants. Very unusual, it had many entrances and exits. Open on all sides. Some of our refugees took advantage of it, just went out without paying. They underestimated the Japanese. The restaurant owners sent a detailed list of food consumed to our committee. When mother and Henry were in Tokyo I went to a Japanese restaurant. Asked first for soup. As they use Soya sauce, one cannot see what is in it. With the first bite I tasted something, no idea what it was, perhaps raw fish or some unknown kind of sea-food. To me, a revolting taste. I just couldn't eat any more. Paid and left. Though it was in Kobe that we got acquainted with sea food and ate it, after this experience I don't touch sea-food of any type, to this very day. Henry does.

It was in Japan that we first realized the importance of knowing English. It was indeed the international language. The amount of English we acquired at the English school in Prague didn't make us professors, yet was enough to teach other refugees to speak that language. Some extra spending money.

The Kushnir brothers came to Kobe. We met a lot. We found a café that charged considerably more for the cup of coffee, but everyone was entitled to choose a classical piece of music. With the four of us we had a full concert program. The owner could produce every piece of music we requested. Once, not remembering the name I wanted to be played, I whistled just a few notes and the café owner recognized it as Haydn's trumpet concerto. The owner, a young man, told us he got the idea from a café in San Francisco. I never saw it San Francisco, though I asked. We went to Japanese theatres, not to plays, but entertainment, dancing. Quite unusual and very colourful.

Kobe was the first place to experience swimming at sea. I did hear the sea has salty water but didn't realize it was that salty. I found out the hard way, having swallowed some, when pulled down by a swirl. Very frightening experience. Stopped me from ever going again far from shore.

The abacus I came across quite frequently in Russia. In Japan that was the computer at the time. Bank tellers used it at such speeds, could never follow them.

The Greeks were giving the Italians a hard time. German help to the Italians in Greece was delayed by the plucky Yugoslavs. How I wish the Czechs had acted that way. It may have made a hell of a difference. Maybe, who knows ? The Yugoslavs were in a much tougher position but they fought !

The first bright side of this war, as O'Connors defeated Graziani's far superior Italian force. The way was now open to Tripoli and to end the war in Libya. Came Churchill with the great idea to weaken O'Connors and have most of his forces shipped to help the Greeks. This, at a time of the Germans' height of power. Sacrificed soldiers to play futile political games as he did throughout the war with disastrous concequences.

Barbarossa soon after took us by surprise. One good thing, England got a respite from German air raids. Not just us, the world held its breath. Experts gave the Russians a chance to hold out just a couple of months. Some thought the German conquest could take as long as three months. No western media gave the Russians a chance to hold out longer than that. Churchill's speech, offered aid to the Soviets, a reversal of his anti-communist past. Jerczy, the older of the Kushnir brothers argued the Russians should not accept help from capitalistic countries. I agreed with the younger brother to be more pragmatic. *Accept assistance from any source.* The Germans advanced deep into Russia at a tremendous speed, we became pessimistic. It seemed the world strategists are right. What then ? Once the Germans defeat Russia, England will stand no chance.

Matsuoka, Japan's foreign minister, went to the United States to make an agreement. Asked to stop USA embargo of strategic raw material. He returned empty-handed and the military took over. Two friends we had made from the Kyoto's Imperial University (one spoke Russian, the other English) warned us there would be war now and we should try to get out of Japan. We were having a good time. We made friends in college. Two visited us in London after the war. It was easy to find us, having given them father's address which did not change. Cathleen, a classmate, Filipino girl, visited us frequently in London after the war. She was stewardess on a Hong-Kong airline. Jack, half Japanese, didn't want to return to Japan. He was an officer in the Japanese army. He saw too much inhuman behaviour by the Japanese soldiers. He soon found the extreme bias against Japanese. Though in Japan he looked European, in Europe he looked Japanese. He had no chance to be accepted anywhere. He returned to Japan and attained a high position at the enormous Japanese concern Nichimen. He arranged for Henry to be sole distributer for the company's cotton yarns for Canada.

We befriended two boys and their family, the Mizrahis. They lived in an adjacent building in Kobe. After the war they moved to Panama.

Our aim was to get to England. John, a friend from the Canadian Academy was the son of the English consul in Kobe. We visited him frequently. His father knew about our predicament. He also knew we have English visas. One day John's father came up with an idea. *Your aim must be to reach Shanghai. Japanese liners sail there regularly. At the British Embassy in Shanghai is a Czech Military Mission. They have the right to enlist you into the Czech army.* The problem, how to get permission to land in Shanghai. *For that some-one in Shanghai must ask for you.* He knew of a solution, but we had to decide. *The Quakers have a hostel in Shanghai. They can ask for you. The condition is, to be baptized to their religion. There is a Quaker priest in Kobe who can baptize you.* We discussed the idea with mother. We understood the tension between the USA and Japan could lead to war. Principles aside, if this is a way to reach England, let's go ahead. Our conversion was a simple procedure – a Quaker priest sprinkled some water on us, we had to repeat a few sentences and the three of us were christened. My Jewish name Salo, was changed to James. Henry was able to keep his name, so could mother, Regina. Soon after our conversion, the request from Shanghai reached us.

This time we travelled on a big Japanese liner. We saw one of these big liners before. Henry befriended a Japanese naval officer, who took us on board to show us the beauty of Japanese ship construction. Very impressive!

In Shanghai, we lived in the Quakers' hostel, 382 Avenue Joffre, in the French concession. There also was an American and British concession. The big part of Shanghai was occupied by the Japanese. One could go over to the Japanese side, but it meant standing in line for hours, to get an anti something injection. Once one joined the queue, no way to get out of it. We considered all, but too curious, to let such an inconvenience change our mind. We were the only European faces in the long line. The Japanese probably used the same needle to inject hundreds or thousands of visitors. We survived.

There were quite a number of Jewish refugees in Shanghai, many from Vienna. We used the streetcar often and not like Europeans generally, we used the cheaper class carriage with the Chinese. Henry and I decided to go to the native Chinese quarter. It was a new experience. Narrow streets, full of people, masses of people. Sitting, walking. We tried very hard to remember the way we came. With no street signs we lost our way easily. With the hand language we made ourselves understood. The Chinese understood, smiled and were very helpful to make us find the part of Shanghai we knew.

The Quakers had two daughters about our age. Asked them to come with us to a cinema. *We don't go to places of entertainment.* Part of their and our adopted religion. Out of the movie, the streets were all flooded. Drainage was not the best in Shanghai. Against our principles we took a rickshaw back to the hostel. The girls laughed. *God punished you.*

September 1, 1941, exactly two years after the Germans started the war, attacking Poland, Henry and I went to register at the Military Mission, to join the Czech army. We were interviewed by English and then by a Czech officer, Captain V.G. Tausig. Checked out, accepted and registered. They told us we would set sail for England the same month. They confiscated our passports. We were now entirely in their hands.

Came the moment we had been dreading. Henry and I had to separate from Mother. We escaped together over the border to Poland. Went together through the hell of Warsaw, walked together to escape to Russia, 20 months through Bialystock, Vilna, Moscow, Vladivostok, Kobe, and finally Shanghai. We hoped we left mother in safe hands, the Quaker hostel. And mother was a plucky woman.

Mother stayed on another year on her own. All that time with the Quakers. She worked in the hostel as a waitress. Although the hostel was in the International Concession, this changed when Japan entered the war in December 1941. Mother was continually in touch with the British Consulate. When she heard a Red Cross steamer was going to evacuate British women and children, she fought to gain a place on that ship. Having sent two boys to England to fight, helped. She succeeded to be taken on board. September 1942, the Red Cross ship headed straight for Lawrenco Marques, capital of Portuguese

Mozambique. There, all the passengers were divided into groups, according to their final destinations. They were guided by volunteer hostesses. The hostess meeting mother, spoke to her in English, which mother was not good at. Mother not only discovered that this hostess also spoke German, but that she was the fiancé of Leo Kalb, the son of a Teplitzer Rabbi.

Mother left Lawrenco Marques on a British liner and reached Liverpool in mid-November 1942 where our relieved father met her.

Quite a feat. A family of five, split in three groups was together again after three years. And that in the middle of the war.

By mid-September 1941, Henry and I were two of a group of thirteen Czech Jewish boys who set sail under the auspices of the British army. The boat was a small freighter, not at all comfortable. The Captain gave us a very friendly welcome. Our first stop was Singapore, where they put us in an Australian army camp. Before we went to sleep that night, one of the Aussies gave us a tip, how to behave in a tropical country. *Take at least two blankets and cover yourself over the head, if you want to stay healthy. If you perspire, that's o.k. The most important thing is to cover your stomach.* We listened to his advice.

We sank into an exhausted  sleep, only to be woken a few hours later to shouts of *get up, get up, out, out* ! There had been some mix-up with our papers. We were no longer allies. They put us on a small boat and a short time later we landed on St. Johns Island, an internment island near Singapore, so small that it took us precisely forty-five minutes to walk the island's circumference.

Apart from our group there were some Vichy French on the island from Indo-China, but they were kept behind barbed wire separate from us. While they sorted out our papers we had six weeks on a *paradise* island! We were supposed to be interned, but what lovely internment. All day just in bathing suits. We all lived in one huge tent. Straw filled mattresses on iron beds and mosquito net protection. We had a Chinese cook, who summoned us to every meal with a huge gong. We lazed away the days, sunbathing and swimming. We could see Singapore. The only way to get there was through shark-infested waters. Nobody tried! Why should we. Never had it so good. For our comfort, the British had fenced off a small area of the sea near the shore, so we could swim unperturbed by sharks. Medusas found their way in. Their sting not very pleasant.

This small island had a Governor. A nice house with a tennis court. And a nice and friendly daughter, two years younger than myself. She was only too happy to have found a tennis partner. I played with her almost every day. The Czech community in Singapore heard about us, provided us with books, in English. Good way to improve that language. They were all employees of the big Czech shoe concern Bata. This concern had rubber plantations near Singapore.

We were really sorry to leave. After six weeks, back to Singapore to board a ship. Now bound for South Africa. It was a Dutch liner, the Subajak from the Dutch East Indies. Dutch crew. Among the passengers, Yugoslav navy officers, Serbs and Bosnians, aiming, like us, to join the war in Europe. Not very difficult to understand each other language wise. We became good friends on our very long journey. A Bosnian officer gave me a watch. I didn't have one since my Doxa financed my brother's trip to Kaunas. The Dutch officers spoke English. The atmosphere on that boat was like a family cruise.

On this stretch to South Africa we saw dolphins for the first time in our life. For hours they kept on following the ship, displaying some artistic and elegant jumps.

We docked in Durban in October. The boat had engine trouble. We didn't think the Dutch crew was in a great hurry to leave the pleasant stay in Durban. So we had another few weeks of good fun. Our boat was like a floating hotel. We slept there and returned for meals. The rest of the time we spent in Durban, a modern city with 50% of the population Indians. The boat had its own bakery that produced the typical English white bread, which the local community seemed to prefer to their own more nutritious one. War time conditions were the reason no white bread was baked, or so we were told. Daily, we took loafs of bread to our South African friends. Enhanced our popularity.

A German Jewish family, many years in Durban, invited us, Henry and me, to dinner. They had already adopted the white South Africans prejudice against the blacks. We had some very fiery arguments.

By mere chance I met an English nanny who looked after David Gandhi's children. David was the great Gandhi's son. David Gandhi was the publisher of a daily newspaper *The Indian Opinion*, aimed at the local Indian community. Had dinner at Gandhi and tasted curry for the first time. Then it was much too spicy for me.

The English nanny introduced me to her friends, who turned out to be the communist leaning white members of the *Non-European United Front*. With one exception, all of them were Jewish. The exception was a lovely girl, Lesley de Villiers of the original Dutch settlers. Together we illegally visited black villages, witnessed demonstrations. Although apartheid wasn't as strong then as it was to become later, I saw enough to give me the creeps. Blacks couldn't travel on the same buses with whites. I once witnessed an elderly white man hitting a black man with a cane, pushing him off the pavement. I went to meetings of the *Non-European United Front*. A British sergeant joined our group.

A student of anthropology took me for an outing to a native village. The home we entered was of the igloo type, probably considerably bigger than the Eskimo igloos. It was obvious she was well known by the natives. As a welcome, we were served a grape juice from dried grapes hanging at the low ceiling. It was served in a coconut shell. My guide told me it is polite to drink it all. I did. Drank it like a medicine. No ill effect.

I was suddenly sympathetic to a world I hated – *democracy*. After the experience we had in Europe with so-called democratic countries, 'democracy' was a dirty word. But here, in South Africa, I saw the blacks fighting for it.

In Durban we were introduced to milk shakes. Love with the first sip. The very positive change we experienced in South Africa, access to international media. No more relying on rumours. We could read and listen to the news. Strongly anti-Soviet. The first time I came across *the Germans should drown in Russian blood*.

Though I know now, the Germans didn't have it easy in the Soviet Union from day one, we were not aware of it then. We only heard of the fast German progress. The first good news from that front, when a Russian counter attack recaptured Rostov in November. Where are the experts now, who predicted the longest Russia could last, was; three months! Whilst it was any day now for the Germans to enter the Soviet capital, came Pearl Harbour. We had left the Far East just over a month before that. The Japanese were now in all of Shanghai, no more foreign concessions. What will this mean for mother ?

The Blitz Krieg that worked so well in Poland and France came to an end in Russia. On the Moscow front the Germans are now in full retreat. I was asked to a party organized by the Non-European United Front to celebrate Germany's defeat. Premature ? Even then I didn't think so. If Rostov was the first sign something is not going according to plan with the German plan, the retreat near Moscow showed a definite turning point. The war continued but the Germans had no longer a chance. Apart from the failure in Russia, the mighty USA industrial power entered the war.

Our two months in Durban came to an end. Our group now split. Seven, who served in the Czech army before the war continued to the Middle East, Palestine. The younger six (including Henry and myself) continued with the same vessel, the Subajak to Capetown.

All six of us met again at the first Czech Army camp in Leamington Spa. Only one, Benedik, came to the 311 RAF squadron, as Henry and I. He was a radio/radar operator. Didn't survive the war. Crashed on an operational flight. None of the crew survived.

We spent seven glorious days in Capetown, thanks to the Czech Consul. We were wined and dined. Were taken to the famous Table Mountain, where monkeys climbed all over our car. Took a number of sight-seeing tours. Were told Cape Town has the highest percentage of Mulattos. We were invited to one of their parties Very pretty girls.

Even good things come to an end. January 1, 1942, my birthday, we set sail for England. To avoid U-boats, the Subajak had to take a very circuitous route, so far west that we saw the coast of Brazil. There were numerous U-boat alarms but the Subajak was a very fast boat. It was a lone runner, without an escort. Very usual for such ships. Jan 25 we landed in Liverpool. We were checked out, flooded with questions, then by train to London. Back to internment. Far cry from the Singapore island experience. Now it was a prison. We only went to our cells to sleep, the rest of the day in one big community room. All nationalities. A French submarine commander was fuming. He had defected to the British with his submarine. *Now he is in jail!*

We were kept there till January 30th. Released, we were given ten days of freedom then to report to our Czech army unit. Father picked us up and after a long, long time we were again in our own home. A house in Hampstead Garden Suburbs. We had not seen each other since

August 1939. Steffi had been evacuated out of London with thousands of other British schoolchildren to a school in St. Albans, Hertfordshire. Mother was still in Shanghai with the Quakers.

To celebrate our reunion, Father took us to his favourite Chinese restaurant in Soho. Introduced us to the owner and said his two sons, China experts, will order the meal. We didn't have a clue about Chinese food. We had steered clear of it in Shanghai; we only ate at the hostel, good American food. Shanghai was too dirty to eat out. Sandwiches sold in kiosks could hardly be seen, covered with a multitude of flies. It was already during Mao's time that flies disappeared. Could not imagine Shanghai without flies.

All too soon we had to report to the army camp. Our real contribution to World War II was about to begin.

# Chapter 6: we join the Royal Air Force

We joined a Czech army camp in Leamington Spa. When we registered, the officer advised everyone to take a cover name so our families wouldn't suffer if we were captured. My brother jumped at the idea. With no time to think, Apfelbaum became Arton. Later my brother changed his name officially by deed poll. We were allocated uniforms; our basic training was to begin. Not before a pet talk by an officer, not friendly description of our duties. When he said *don't think being intellectuals, you'll have any privileges.* I interrupted, *you actually meant to say Jews, not intellectuals?* This started my army service with a 7 days detention. I had to do a lot of extra work, peeling potatoes, cleaning and sleep separately. Still it had taught this officer a lesson. He lost his nasty tone.

Being sportsmen, we were not deterred by the tough physical training; in fact enjoyed it. Henry developed an ingrown toe nail and was hospitalized in Shakespeare's Stratford-upon-Avon. Lying in a hospital bed, Henry obviously had time to think. When I came to see him, he said: we are enjoying ourselves here, all the physical training and so on. We are not killing anyone – yet. But once we leave here and really start fighting, we can be in a situation where a German soldier confronts us and we have to kill him. Whoever shoots first, will kill the other. He might beg us not to shoot *three children depend on me.* We may hesitate. In that split second, he will fire. *That is not for us. Those not understanding German haven't got that problem.*

*So what do you suggest? We can't leave the army.* His answer *Let's transfer to the air force. There we drop bombs. We don't see anybody, we don't know who we kill.* I wasn't too keen on the idea, but as we were close and I didn't want to be separated from my brother, I agreed to put in an application with him. We were both accepted. We had served in the army for only two months.

The differences between serving in the army and the air force were immediately apparent. One felt in an *elite* force. Although we still had to queue for our food, but unlike the army where the food was all slopped together in two metal containers and in the open air, using the lap as one's table, in the air force we ate in a huge dining room, called *mess*. We used proper plates and decent cutlery. There I had bacon for the first time and love it ever since.

Our first base was a transit camp in St. Athens, near Cardiff, southern Wales. There we kept on waiting to be selected to which function one is suitable. I utilized some of this free time constructively. As my studies had been interrupted, I decided to study to pass matriculation exams. The science subjects, math and physics, were easy, but I had to study English, language and literature, and a foreign language. As   a Czech National I was not allowed to take Czech as a foreign language, I took German, which I knew just as well. I passed the exams easily.

The camp was huge, housing some 20,000 people. It was like a city, a city spread over an enormous area, because the huts were placed far apart as a precaution against air attacks. I soon became friendly with other Czech boys who were already stationed there. Here I got to know Lada Novak. We became best friends throughout the war. Lada had fought in Spain, the Spanish Civil War. Then the Czech Army in France and came to England at Dunkirk. Lada was an exceptional character. Very level headed. Every word was well thought out. After the war, back in Czechoslovakia we stayed together till I was posted to Liberec and he to Brno. When I was back in Prague he came to see me frequently. Our final split, when I returned to England. When Lada was asked for his pre-war occupation *dělnik z Modřan*. Modřany, near Prague.

Back to St. Athens. Whilst waiting to start our specific courses, with Lada we came upon the idea to form a discussion group. Subjects to be discussed, current affairs and historical events. However, it was against British army rules to hold political discussions. We needed a sponsor and a *legal* place where to meet. The first man we approached was the Czech liaison officer, lieutenant

Kraus. He simply told us it was illegal and we couldn't do it. Next, we turned to the protestant Minister, the Air Force Chaplain. Little did I know this man would influence my way of thinking so much. From this army chaplain I learned the real meaning of tolerance. A most remarkable man. He agreed to our request, calling our group a study group. He stipulated only one condition, every fourth discussion to be on a religious subject. He provided a venue, the church auditorium. The minister would be our moderator.

From this wise, gentle man, I learned a lot. To listen and to respect another person's views. The minister didn't stop us from discussing any subject. The most touchy, *should Chamberlain and his appeasers be found guilty for the outbreak of the war.* Together with a few of us the minister participated in planning subjects to be discussed. One of the group got the job of preparing the chosen subject and presenting it. We found England much behind the Continent in theatres, operas, concert halls. In most places, even big towns, these just did not exist. Yet their libraries were unique. We made good use of them to prepare our discussions. More than a hundred boys usually attended. This unforeseen large number; thanks to the minister. And thanks to the minister we were legally protected.

We enjoyed social life as well. We were friendly with the local people, attended dances, parties, celebrations and to entertain their daughters. One night I was invited to a party in Cardiff. As I got there, a thick fog blanketed the city. Visibility was practically nil, and the darkness and the blackout didn't help. I couldn't find the address I was looking for. A girl emerged out of the hazy darkness and invites me to a party. In those days everyone was friendly. So I went along. As I got there, I couldn't belief my eyes. This was the party I had been looking for, and my friends were all there.

A few of us visited Pontypridd, invited by the owners of a big zipper factory. They were natives of Plzen.

After some three months of waiting, we were given psychometric tests and had interviews to decide on our future jobs. Henry was astigmatic; therefore was not allowed to fly. Instead he was trained as a high grade aircraft mechanic, a fitter. I wanted to be a pilot. Doesn't everybody want to be a pilot when joining an Air Force ? After the tests, I was told they wanted me to be a navigator. I was very disappointed, but the officer in charge explained that they needed every boy, good in mathematics, to be a navigator on heavy bombers. The navigator is the brain of the crew.

At first, pilots and navigators trained together. Each had to know a certain amount about the other's work. The navigators were from many countries; everyone had to have a good standard of English. All the training was in that language. Unlike the Poles, we didn't have our own

Air Force. There were four   Czech squadrons, part of the R.A.F. We wore RAF uniforms. Our RAF identity card bore a stamp *Czechoslovakia.*

Our first training course, in a luxurious hotel at the seaside resort of Eastbourne, now empty of visitors. We didn't stay there very long. German fighter planes decided to use us for shooting practice. They approached the coast at sea level, to avoid being detected, fired a few shells and turned back! Too dangerous! We were transferred to the north, to Harrogate. A very fashionable holiday resort, not far from Leeds. Even more beautiful than the Eastbourne one. Very posh hotel. In peace time I imagine the service was slightly better.

Our next camp was in a place called Bridgenorth near Wolverhampton. The camp was actually a girls' camp, housing 5000 air force girls. We were a small group of navigator cadets in a far corner of the camp. I remember Wolverhampton, a place with probably the worst climate. I don't think people living there ever saw the sun! Rain or rather drizzle most of the time.

One day, after a few days' leave in London, I arrived in Wolverhampton at the crack of dawn. It was still dark. Wrapped in my air force coat with the collar high up for warmth, I waited for the air force bus to take me to camp. Someone approached me and said,

*We need a tenth for a minion.*

*How do you know I am   Jewish?*

I don't. I take my chances. If you don't understand what I mean, you're not. Jewish.

Unfortunately I couldn't help out, there only was one bus to camp.

The navigational studies, just the theory of *dead reckoning.* Why we use the Mercator type chart for navigation, (introduced by a Flemish Geographer in 1569). Meteorology. Variations and deviations. The compass. The Morse code. Astronavigation, how to use the stars as navigational aids. How to measure wind speed over the ocean, when no other system available. The use of the sextant. The use of the radio for navigation. Radar. The bomb sight. The theory of hitting a target. How to fold our own parachutes. How to repair our instruments in mid air. How to navigate when taking evasive action. The language to use communicating to each other in mid air. How to speak to the control tower.

Had I known how stormy the Irish Sea is I would have preferred to swim. We were taken by boat to the Isle of Man. Our base: Jurby. The extreme north/east part of the island. I only knew about the Isle of Man as a place on the map. Quite an interesting experience. It has a narrow gauge railroad, also the wagons are smaller. Never heard of Manx cats before. They have no tail. The island was still at war since 1914. Never signed a peace agreement in 1918. The best brake, the island had no food rationing. In England one couldn't get a meal for more than five shilling. The more expensive restaurants found a way to increase the bill. They charged for the use of the table cloth, of the cutlery, the plates. The chairs and the tables were for free !

The first evening on the island, with Berman, Lenhoff, Mandler we were off to the capital, Douglas, on that mini-train. The object, to experience the feeling of having a meal with no restrictions. All we needed was to find a decent restaurant. But how ? No-one in the streets, a strange place and the black-out. We came across a big hotel. This must have a dining room! The entrance also half dark. There was an oversized door, this could be it. I entered first. The door not yet fully open, I saw a very large room, it had probably been the dining room, but not now. There were no tourists. At the far corner, high army officers sat at a big conference table. Before I managed to close the door, one of the officers called; Salo come in ! In his uniform I couldn't recognize him at first. He was the British consul from Kobe. He was the one who gave us the idea how to get out from Japan via Shanghai, to enlist there at the British Embassy. He was very happy to see me in uniform, also that Henry was in the RAF. After all, it was thanks to him that we left the Far East in time. I inquired about John, his son, our classmate at Kobe's Canadian Academy. Because of his knowledge of Japanese he stayed in the Far East in an intelligence unit.

Now we had some-one to give us directions to a good restaurant.

Our first practice flights were on Oxfords. A two motor flimsy contraption. Every time we took off I thought I'll be sick. Started to doubt if flying is at all for me. Couldn't stand the strong smell of petrol. It passed.

At the end of the course, we got our navigators' wings and promoted to sergeants.

Not like today, when even heavy aircraft are directed by ground control. Then, a navigator, once in the air, was on his own. It was for the navigator to direct the way to the target, for the navigator, to direct the pilot back to base. We learned how to navigate by day and night with no help from ground control. The additional difficulty at night was the stringent blackout throughout the British isles. Even in total darkness we learned to distinguish between rivers, lakes from dry land. Recognize the presence of towns by the mist and smoke in the area. Learn how to decipher coded messages at top speed. Everything in the air depends on speed. The codes were changed every two hours, for security reasons. Crew co-operation was vital. We learned some of the radio and radar operators' tasks. Get correct bearings, to recognize targets or pin-points. Visual observation, mainly by the gunners, should be correct, most important when sighting an enemy aircraft. Mutual trust between the first pilot and navigator was a must. We were in a situation that this has come to the test. We survived. We studied ship-recognition. All war-ships by their classes. How to estimate the size of freighters, liners, banana ships. How not to lose track when pilots had to exercise evasive action, when pursued by enemy aircraft. Not very pleasant, nor healthy and no easy additional task for the navigator. What if the aircraft is hit by lightning or another reason for instruments to go out of control. Best solution to turn to Astro-Navigation providing the overcast is not too thick. We were provided with astro-maps in the form of a round calculator to show which star should appear in which part of the sky at a certain time. This facilitated to recognize a single star, without seeing the constellation to which it belongs. Very important for the ever-clouded Western European sky. The other problem was the inaccuracy of the sextant. The naval navigators were able to find the ship location within a mile or two. They knew their exact height thus also the ships angle to the horizon, therefore took precise angles of stars. We never knew our exact height. The altimeter was set by the air pressure at our base. Much later we got radar altimeters, but these were only used for landing, giving the real height over the runway. Not knowing our height we had to use a bubble sextant. For the sextant there was a small astro dome at the top of my compartment. How to keep a bubble in the centre, to take a reading whilst in flight. Not easy. We therefore took measurements to establish our personal error. Mine was thirty miles. Once when I   was in trouble, due to gale force winds and gusts, I used my error as fifty miles. A safety margin. Most frustrating to perish due to a navigation error.

Henry and I joined the RAF in April 1942. My first operational flight was exactly two years later. For our last training we were sent to the Bahamas islands. This was the O.T.U., Operational Training Unit. We were now training in crews that will stay together for operational flying.

We left England from Liverpool where I had landed with Henry, just some 18 months ago. Now, as we set sail for the New World, Sept 3 1943, Montgomery's Eighth Army landed at the most southerly tip of Italy. More than six months it took the Allied armies to get the Germans out of Africa. Then Sicily. The Russians are already nearing their original borders. Every day freeing more people from the Nazi yoke. The Allies are playing political games. Let more freedom fighters be executed, more people mistreated as slave labourers, more Jews gassed. The Allies landed on the Continent of Europe at the most southerly point of the Apennine peninsula. Not suitable for fast advance, ideal for defence. Millions more had to die for Churchill's and Roosevelt's idiocy.

Our ship was none other than the Queen Elizabeth commissioned for war use. We spent the voyage in the lap of luxury. With just a few hundred aboard, we were treated as first class passengers. We roamed around a lot, admiring the beauty of this luxury liner. The ship was going on its own, not in a convoy. Like all fast boats. The convoys were going at 12miles an hour.

We landed in Halifax, and continued by train and bus to Montreal. Were stationed at Dorval airport. Did nothing but wait. Our spare time we spent in Montreal. After a long time a town without black-out. As though on a different planet. The lights, the neon signs in all colours! How different from the drab looking towns in England. Here war was **only** in the news. Walking in the formal uniform which read Czechoslovakia on both shoulders, an inquisitive well-dressed gentleman approached me. He was the owner of the nightclub, Samovar. Airmen as such were in high esteem. From Czechoslovakia and able to speak Russian, his language, he had to introduce me to his family. I was an invited guest every evening that I came to Montreal. Sat at the family table. Was served excellent food. Next to me, an attractive lady, perhaps mid- thirties. She was an artist, a painter from somewhere in the USA. All very interested what life is like in England, the black-out, the food rationing, about the country I come from, about life in Russia. At the table of some dozen people, both English and Russian was spoken. Madeleine stayed at the posh Hotel, opposite the nightclub, the Mount Royal hotel. After dinner invited me to her room to admire her paintings. That's what we did, admire the paintings!

Naturally, I had to shop. I bought a gold Longines watch for mother and a Longines for myself at Burks. 50 years later, wearing the same watch, I walked into the same shop and showed it to the owner. I don't know what I expected, but all the owner said *nice* and I walked out.

Had to make another call in Montreal. Before I left England, Václav Nosek gave me a Montreal address of a Slovak communist group. I met them one evening. Some twenty, very pleasant and intelligent people bombarded me with a million questions. Told me about their life in Canada. Most had sons and daughters in the Canadian forces in various theatres of war. One of the ladies gave me the telephone number of the head of the dock workers' union in Nassau, the Bahamas. I met him a few times.

By train to Miami, took two days. We were given *K-rations,* a little box with a few concentrated food squares to cut up, one for each meal. What was supposed to be our ration for the whole trip, we ate in one go. At every train stop, we jumped off to buy some real food.

In the middle of the night, the train stopped in Washington. It was scheduled to continue two hours later. What an opportunity to see the White House. Not really the right time. A few of us grabbed a cab and asked to be taken to the White House. The taxi driver was suspicious *what in the middle of the night!* I should mention, in the USA people did not know RAF uniforms.

Anyway, the driver took us    there. It was pitch dark, and we couldn't see anything, but we were able to say, we had been near the White House.

The tiresome train journey was not without its compensation. The adjacent carriage was occupied by American army girls (WACs). I got friendly with one of them, Florence, who I contacted in New York on the way back from the Bahamas. From Miami we went by boat to Nassau, capital of the Bahamas. Our first lecture was by an RAF doctor who warned us to keep away from the local girls. They are all diseased. Some didn't listen to the doctor's advice. They found out the hard way. One English airman even married a local white girl. Soon contracted a venereal disease. Marriage was over.

We arrived at the end of September, and were told only to wear long sleeved shirts. The humidity was so high, the slightest scratch could become infected.

We were stationed on Windsor Field, named after the Duke of Windsor who was governor there. He, as Edward VII, in 1936, gave up the throne of England for the woman he loved. An American divorcée, Mrs Wallis Simpson. She was not particularly pretty, however very nice to us airmen. She ran a canteen with free food and she herself served us. The Duke was very unpopular. Army discipline is very important, particularly in the British Army. But during the war, many of the rules, such as saluting an officer, were relaxed. Not so in the

Bahamas. One day on our notice board, that we have to salute the Duke's car, even if the Duke is not in it. We took it as a bad joke!

The Sunday parade was new to me. The whole camp lines up and waits for the commanding officer. He is not in a hurry. We stood in that heat, in the sun, waiting. Every time a few airmen passed out, sun stroke. As the big boss arrived, a flight/sergeant shouted Jews, Catholics and some other denominations, *two steps forward, turn right, return to barracks*. We were free, didn't have to pray.

Our training in the Bahamas, including travel time, took six months. We sailed September 1943, arriving back in England, the first days of March 1944. All the time crews came, did their training, and then went off to join the war effort. We trained on the B25, a twin-engine aircraft in the same category as the one we were going to fly operationally, the four engine B24. The B-25, the Mitchell, had a Perspex front and that is where my navigator's cubical was. In the Bahamas climate, the heat was unbearable. Not just the heat, the humidity was worse. Wearing just shorts, entering the aircraft, as though a jump into water. Not so easy to hold a pencil, other instruments and work with them. Extremely unpleasant. No choice, had to get used to it. Training had its local dangers. Tornados were very frequent.

We had to climb as quickly   as possible above 2000 feet to avoid being hit by one.

We were training to navigate by night. Can't see a thing, flying over the sea, which from a navigator's point of view, is the most difficult task. No land marks, no pin-points. All one can see from the plane is an inky blackness. We had to rely on dead reckoning. The Oxford Dictionary describes dead reckoning: *calculation of a ship's position from the log, compass, when observation is impossible.*

Whenever we returned from a night flight we went to the Operations Room to see who had come in, and who was overdue. One night, the Palestinians were overdue. A Jewish crew that had come from Palestine. We waited for a while, then organized three planes to go to search for them. We flew in box formation. Each plane is allocated a geographical box. That way we could cover a very big area. We searched for hours, not a clue. The next morning we went out again to see if we could at least see any wreckage. Nothing at all. They completely disappeared. We could only conclude they were struck by a tornado. Petr Brdský, Pavel Fuchs, Rupert Krupica, Miroslav Styblík, Josef Shimandl, Hanuš Tomek. Their names are inscribed on an RAF board in Ottawa (Canada).

Despite our rigorous training, we had some leisure time as well. I was standing at a jetty at the port of Nassau with Adolf Kasal, radio- operator/gunner of our crew, when a man approached us. He heard us speak Czech. He introduced himself in Czech. He was the head doctor of the Bahamas, and his hospital was on Eleuthera Island, a very long and narrow island. He invited us to visit him. We complied a couple of weeks later. Hitched a lift on the weekly provisions boat. Very slow boat with a very noisy engine. A six hours journey. Seeing my navigator's sign on my tunic, the elderly captain, asked me to take the rudder. He showed me a far-away pin-point. Go straight in that direction. I did well till suddenly I saw rocks not very deep below us. Adolf went to wake the captain. He took over, zigzagged away from the rocks and gave me the rudder again till he took over to manoeuvre the boat to the jetty. Our doctor friend found us accommodation in the hospital. We enjoyed our holiday on the island. Young black boys and girls taught us how to dive into the sea and take a ride on the back of giant turtles. An American owner of a banana plantation invited us to his huge mansion for meals every day. Let us use the swimming pool. His 12-year old daughter taught me to swim underwater with eyes open, something I had not mastered before.

In the north of the island there were a number of such plantations, all run by Americans. We visited a number of them. This fruit is transported in very fast *Banana ships*. Bananas don't take to refrigeration and spoil quickly. There were no bananas in England during wartime. The Banana boats   had all been requisitioned by the Navy, in view of their high speed.

In the Bahamas too, we organized a discussion group. When the subject to be discussed was: A critique of the conduct of this war, I and others spoke strongly against the failure of the Allies to open a Second Front in 1942. Present at that talk were, as usual, airmen of various nationalities. Dutch, Belgians, one from Iceland, English and us Czechs. One of the English boys, who never opened his mouth to express his opinion, went to the commanding officer to complain that we expressed anti-government views. The Commander called me to his office. At first in a loud voice, *I will see to it that you get court-martialed.* At that time I didn't yet know that similar views were expressed by leading members of the British government, like Lord Beaverbrook, Sir Stafford Cripps and others. Slowly it turned to a matter of fact discussion. My luck, he was an intelligent man, unlike most high British officers. He agreed this is a new type of war and the strict rule; *no politics in the Army* is obsolete. In the end he dismissed me with; *O.K. go.* Still excited from that experience I helped myself to the, in the Bahamas very cheap alcoholic drinks, to get my composure back. Whisky, brandy and other drinks were just 3 pence, compared to two and a half shillings in England.

I was called again to the Commander's office, when the local dock workers went on strike. Asked me about my visits to the head of the dock workers' union. This time he said with a smile, he was asked to find out, if I had anything to do with it.

For our final exam, we had to locate a very small boat, which had sailed to a certain point about one and a half hours' flying time. There was no other aid, just pure dead reckoning. There was no radio aid, because there were no radio stations to home on. To make it more difficult, just the night on that mission, it was misty. I was so proud to have found that little boat only to learn that all of the navigators did as well. To prove that we found the boat we threw a marker flare. Later, our examiners identified each marker by its colour.

Navigators who achieved high marks, automatically became officers. Our group of eight navigators, all got the necessary high marks. All of us higher than our colleagues from other countries. English, Dutch, Belgian. Yet, in our case the Czech command decided: no officer's rank for us ! All eight of us were Jewish. In Teplice or at high school in Duchcov, I never felt any prejudice on the part of students or teachers, professors. With the professional officers prejudice had not evaporated. During operational flying our ranks increased automatically. Yet whilst we ended the war as Flying Officers, our English co-cadets as Squadron Leaders.

Leaving the Bahamas we were offered to buy the American tropical uniforms that we wore, very cheaply. Nobody did. There was hardly a summer in England, never mind tropical weather.

Back at Dorval we were given a ten-day leave. I seized the opportunity and made my way to New York. I stayed at an RAF hostel and got in touch with Florence.

We were a curiosity to the Americans. They had never seen RAF uniforms, let alone those with a Czech insignia. Wherever I went, I was not charged. The only people who took me for a ride were the barbers. I was charged $1 for a shave, when a very expensive pair of shoes I bought for $3. The others to fix us, the restaurants in Chinatown.

At the Air Force hostel I could get tickets for shows at a reduced price. Florence and I wanted to see the top Norwegian skater, Sonya Heni. She was performing at Madison Square Gardens. Even through the air force club, the tickets were $5 each. A lot of money then.

When we arrived to see the show, we found a mix-up with the dates. Instead of Sonya Heni, an important boxing match was scheduled with the very famous Braddock. I looked at Florence and asked her if she liked boxing. Her expression was enough to tell me. Nor did I. I went to the box office and asked for a refund for the tickets.

*Don't be silly,* so the cashier. *People out there will pay you a much higher price.* I sold those tickets outside Madison Square Gardens for $25 each.

Feeling rich, we went to Jack Dempsey's nightclub on Broadway. Had a wonderful evening, dining and dancing. When it was time to go, I asked for the bill. Jack Dempsey himself brought a folded piece of paper on a plate, what I thought is the bill. In fact it was a note saying *with the compliments of the management.* I went over to Jack Dempsey to thank him.

I took Florence back to her camp by taxi. For me, the night was still young. I took a cab back to Manhattan. After the tension in Europe and living with blackouts for two years, why not use the pleasure of lights. I entered a bar, where I received a warm welcome from all the customers, who insisted on treating me to drinks. It was that night I learned the meaning of a *chaser.* Whiskey (or bourbon as the Americans would say), followed by a small glass of beer. In the end one doesn't know which is chasing what, but I sure got drunk that night!

Some 30 years later, with Sally in New York, wanted to show her Madison Square Gardens. I knew exactly where it was. Never knew it was moved to a different place.

Back to New-York 1944. I heard of the Jewish Serviceman's club, at the main synagogue in Manhattan. I stopped a GI in the street and asked him for directions.

*Come along with me, I'm on the way there.* That he was not American I could hear from his accent. He had come to the USA from Poland and wonders never cease. We discovered, I met both his brothers in Kobe, in 1941.

I couldn't leave New-York without seeing Radio City. A popular show was on. A spotlight was circling, shining at the audience, and wherever the light stopped, the lucky victim went up on stage, answered a few questions and came away with a prize. I wasn't there long, when the spot light stopped throwing the light on me. I climbed to the stage, was asked my name, where I came from and lots of other questions. The moderator then asked me to read a joke. As long as the audience kept on laughing, he threw quarters into a hat. I made signs for the audience to keep on laughing. I came away with $25 in quarters. My mother's cousin from Denver heard the show and wrote to ask if I am her son.

Back then New York was still a safe city. Although warned not to, I went to Harlem. I had no problem there. Just curious people asking about my uniform.

I was very impressed with the Natural Science museum, but most I enjoyed the Planetarium. We were not only shown the night sky, the public was asked to name stars and constellations the speaker pointed out. A US naval officer and I were competing with the answers. He could name many stars I never heard of. After the show, had a very interesting conversation with same officer on that subject. Naval navigators used astronavigation practically all the time, we only as a last resort, when all other means were not available or failed. They could find their position by stars precisely, which we couldn't. To do with the height, the speed, the type of sextant.

Before embarking for the journey back to England, I bought a kitbag, nearly my height. I also had the smaller issued one. Filled them with all sorts of things unavailable in wartime England. Silk stockings, cosmetics etc. All for mother.

From Dorval we now travelled by train to a place called Moncton, where we waited for the boat. Many years later, at an open air event at Kibbutz Givath Hayim I met a Canadian group of youngsters. When I asked them where they came from: *you would never know that small place Moncton, in New Brunswick.* From there it was a short trip to Halifax to board the French liner, the *Ile de France.*

This now was quite different from our journey coming here. The Ile de France was a 55,000 ton luxury liner. No luxury was visible. We joined some 25,000 GIs. Beds in every corner of the ship. Where there was no room for a bed, hammocks. Six of us navigators were lucky to get a cabin for ourselves. What I remember most about that voyage, being hungry and thirsty all the time. Imagine trying to feed 25,000 people! The kitchen was serving 24 hours a day. Everyone was provided with two meal tickets per day, and whatever time was on that ticket, one had to keep. Mine was 3am and 3pm. Those were the hours I could get food. That's it. And the food, all in one container. To wash, only at a fixed time of the day, the rest of the day there just was no water. The water wasn't so pleasant either; sea water. The Americans passed the time playing cards: crap, poker, you name it. And they played for money, a lot of money. Some guys lost all they had. Cheating was part of the game.

To avoid German U-boats, we travelled north towards Greenland, before turning south towards the English port of Liverpool. Also this time, we were not in a convoy and had no escort.

The voyage took ten days. On arrival, we were told to report to an RAF base in Wales, Beaulieu. Our squadron wasn't there at all. Not a compliment to RAF organization. Back to the train for the long journey to the extreme end of Cornwall, Predannack. Henry was there. Henry at a Czech squadron. He spoke Czech! No idea where he got it from. He never learned it. The courses, were all in English, which we both learned in Prague. Together we spoke German throughout the war. We decided to rent a room in the nearby village, Mullion, to use in our free time. It was in a single family house, where Mrs Landry lived with her seven year old daughter.

Czechoslovakia had four squadrons within the framework of the Royal Air Force. 310, 312, 313 were fighter squadrons, flying Spitfires. Ours the 311 was the only bomber squadron. We flew the Boeing B24, (in England named the *Liberator*) a four engine aircraft. After the older types, two and four engine bombers went out of commission, three types of four engine aircraft prevailed, The American B17, Flying Fortress, the American B24, Liberator and the British Lancaster. The total production figure of each of these during the war was in the region of 17,000. The Flying Fortress had only American crews and used for daylight bombing. The Lancaster had British crews and mainly active in night raids. The B24 was flown by U.S as well as British crews. Some were part of Bomber Command, some, as our squadron, of Coastal Command. We were trained for anti-U-boat warfare.

Our crew consisted of the basic six, who trained together in the Bahamas. First pilot, second pilot, flight mechanic, navigator, 2 radio/radar operators. For operational flights we had added three to four boys, not necessarily always the same. Positions to be occupied all the time; two pilots, navigator, flight mechanic, radio, radar, front gun, top gun, rear gun. 2 side guns, in the rear section of the fuselage, only when needed. The radio and radar operators had to change positions frequently.

The flight mechanic had to keep an eye on the proper functioning of the engines, check petrol and oil consumption. On flights of fifteen hours, we had just a half an hour's petrol reserve. When for unforeseen reasons had to use emergency boosts, when trying to evade fighter planes, the petrol consumption jumped. May also jump for undetermined reasons, like being hit by enemy fire. Mechanics had to check if it caused a petrol or oil leak, hydraulic problem.

The radio operator had to listen in to possible instructions or information. He had to keep radio silence unless already sighted by the enemy or in an emergency. Also to give radio bearings as an aid for the navigator.

It is good crew co-ordination that gave a better chance to survive. We were very young, most in the very early twenties, responsible for our and the crew's lives and the war effort.

Our squadron was originally assigned to Bomber Command, flying the twin engine Wellingtons. This must have been one of the worst aircraft used in WWII. Fortunately, by the time I arrived, the squadron had already been equipped with the B24.

Before the first flight it was tradition to break a mirror. This was supposed to bring seven years of bad luck. It didn't work for everybody.

I started operational flying in April 1944, when preparations for the invasion of mainland Europe were in full swing. Although we were just a year away for the war to end, German defences became strongest during that year. It is that year the Germans also built their Western Wall. Also the number of planes, anti-aircraft guns had increased considerably during that year. We guessed the Allies will not be able to find new devices to make the war drag on, as the Russians were already nearing the German border.

The introduction of the four-engine heavy bomber, which could be airborne fifteen hours, gave anti-U-boat warfare an enormous advantage. With less aircraft a 24 hour surveillance was possible. The main ports of exit to the Atlantic were in the Bay of Biscay. These ports became our prime targets. The Germans introduced the Schnorkel, a miniature chimney, which enabled the combustion engines to continue running whilst the boat was submerged. Yet the Germans fitted only a limited number of U-boats with this gadget. The U-boat's electric engine had a short time limit.

In good weather, our radar operators learned to recognize the surf patterns left by the schnorkel and we could aim our depth charges accurately. When the weather was bad, we just dropped the depth charges at anything that looked suspicious. Once the long distance Liberator joined the anti-U-boat warfare, the U-boats could no longer come out singly to the open Atlantic. The Germans devised a new method, they came out in groups of three. As we attacked at low level, 50 feet during the day, 200 feet when dark, we would be too easy targets for a group of U-boats. Therefore orders were, not to attack in such cases. We had to keep a safe distance, call for Beaufighters' support and let them home on us. As the Germans saw the fast twin-engine monsters approaching, the U-boats submerged and rushed back to port.

Our success, in severely limiting U-boat operations is vividly described in the book *Iron Coffins* by a former U-boat commander Herbert A. Werner.

Often the U-boats came out with air support. They used the twin engine Junkers 88. We couldn't fight them. Our defense, to go down to sea level. The guns of the Fighter aircraft are in the bow. As we flew that low, they couldn't attack. Not enough space to pull up again. Our machine guns had 0.5 inch cartridges, compared to 0.33 on British aircraft.

For calculations in the air we used something like a slide-ruler, but in a round form. It simply worked faster than the usual straight ruler, yet not as exact. In the air, speed has an advantage over accuracy. We, navigators, were issued these very good rulers, *Made in Germany !!* We were also given very good watches Omega and Longines. Everyone checked his watch for accuracy. The maximum 24 hours error should not exceed four seconds. The error had to be constant, to be  able to tell the exact time. Very important for astro-navigation.

Our first operational flight was with our squadron leader in the first pilot's seat, and the navigation instructor next to me. Our destination: the Bay of Biscay. As if to order, as we approached we spotted three U-boats leaving their port to make their way to the open Atlantic. Ludek called the feared Beaufighters who came and spoiled their fun. The Junkers 88 was no match to the Beaufighter.

Though we trained in the Bahamas to navigate at sea without an opportunity of any pinpoints, these flights were not longer than two hours. Now, we only saw water for 5 or 6 hours. The last pinpoint we saw on our way out were the Scilly Isles and those isles were the first land we spotted on our return flights. We navigated by dead reckoning, checked our positions with radio bearings. We used the very reliable German radio aids, set up for the U-boats. Blatchley Park scientists broke the enemy codes. Wind speed and direction we measured by the direction of the eddies .

Operational flights were usually planned well in advance. We did not *scramble* like the fighter crews. We knew we would be flying for a period of ten to fifteen hours; day overlapped into night and vice versa. First in the procedure was the briefing with all the crews participating in that specific mission. A commander would give us the place and purpose of the mission, an intelligence officer would tell us where we might encounter enemy opposition, provide us with the codes and at what time these would be changed. He also informed us which wavelengths to use, and which colour flares would enable us to identify a friendly boat. We were given the codes the Germans were using as navigational aids, for us to use as well. Finally we were briefed by the meteorologist who gave us the weather report for our and the target area including possible changes in the force and direction of the wind. Many times he did not tell us the truth, when very bad weather was expected.

Should we have to bail out, over enemy territory, we were told to go to peasants for help they were more likely to be anti-German. Never to rich houses. The Resistance movements in France and Belgium were left-wing. Rich people were more likely to be collaborators .

After the briefing, we would eat. We Czechs had our own kitchen with Czech cooks, who cooked for us all the Czech specialties. This dining room was used only for outgoing and returning crews. We called this meal, *The Last Supper*. As we left, we were given *'food for our journey'* – sandwiches, and coffee in vacuum flasks. The coffee was laced with a stimulant.

For every six junior officers there was a batman who cleaned our shoes pressed our gala uniforms and polished the buttons on those. For us Czechs, this was something oh so English, even though our batmen were Czechs.

Every six weeks we had ten days leave to enable us to relax from the strain. This was a very welcome rest. After each mission, we all waited anxiously to check if the other planes came back. At the beginning, all the guys were virtual strangers. After training together for many months, we became close friends. With our youthful bravado we thought at first, nothing can happen to us. But as it did to our closest friends, our views became much more pragmatic.

We normally slept two to a room, Before a flight all outgoing crews slept in one big room, which reminded me of a hospital ward. I could never sleep the night before a flight. We had to sleep fully clothed, including boots. Sometimes we were just on standby. We could not be left on standby for more than 24 hours. On one of those standby nights when I couldn't sleep and was thinking what a coward I must be compared to everyone else, I heard someone cough. Aren't you asleep? I said into the darkness, to no one in particular. No, I can never sleep before an operational flight, came the answer. And then everyone in the room started to talk. So it was not just me.

Of course it was not very good to start a 15 hour operation when tired, which with food, briefing and debriefing was nearer to 18 hours. But once we were airborne, the tiredness vanished. We concentrated on the mission. It was usually on the home run as we came near to base, began to relax a bit, that was when tiredness kicked in.

Only occasionally did someone panic. In the RAF anyone who said he was afraid, did not have to fly again. Being afraid, becomes a liability to the rest of the crew. If this happened in the course of the first operations, the airman would be demoted and given a non-flying job. But if the fear was as a result of traumatic experience after many flights, he had a chance to get another, non-flying job, but not be demoted.

During the flight it was the navigator's job to record everything in the logbook: every change of weather, every change of direction, when and where we were attacked. Any sightings, of our and enemy navy units, even fishing boats. We were not expected to approach friendly naval vessels. They would fire at us even if we were to fire the correct flare. We reported marked and unmarked anti- aircraft positions, wind changes. In short, we had to enter everything we came across. Most of all to plot our position and tell the pilots which direction to take. The longest period between entries usually not more than two minutes. Thus, if one wandered off course could look back and hopefully, find the mistake and rectify it.

Irreversible mistakes were made of course and a number of planes were lost due to navigational errors.

We usually returned in the early hours of the morning. At the end of a mission, the whole crew went off to eat breakfast, while the first pilot and the navigator went for debriefing, which could last more than an hour. Any new and useful information we could provide was passed on to Intelligence. My log entries were analysed. After the debriefing we went to eat. Then we played snooker. An excellent way to relax. We usually played until the official breakfast time, then ate again.

After a mission, as a rule, we had two days off. Whilst others played cards, sat in the mess, drank, talked, we navigators spent time in the intelligence room, reading reports of other navigators. They reported unmarked defence positions, the accuracy or inaccuracy of ours or German navigational aids, unusual compass deviations etc. Also about things that went wrong.

An extreme case of navigational error. A navigator made the mistake of plotting the wind direction **with**, instead of **against** the wind. When, after some hours he discovered the mistake, sent out SOS, asking for his position. The aircraft was by then too far away from any land base. Not enough petrol to reach it.

On our flights, we came across Spanish fishing boats in the Bay of Biscay. As some of them were aiding the Germans, we chased them off with machinegun fire.

One problem we often had to contend with, whilst returning to base, was the infamous English fog. In one of the extreme cases, our ground control told us we could not land at our base at Predannak, as the fog was too thick and too low. Our radar was not yet sufficiently accurate to guide us. There was at that time no such thing as a blind landing. Later in the war there was a primitive form of blind landing where a beam was directed towards us and we had to remain within the boundaries of the beam. In the last minute, or few seconds, the pilot saw the ground and carried out the landing procedure.

So there we were flying over the English Channel. On our port side the English coast with the dangerous barrage balloons, starboard the coast of France. We made use of an instrument called IFF – *Identification Friend or Foe*. The usual procedure was to switch this instrument off as we left British air space, on our outward flight. Returning, switched it on again 100 kilometres before the British coast. By using this instrument, coastal defences knew a British plane was coming in. Yet on this particular flight, flying through the English Channel we activated it though the enemy could also detect it. The reason we switched it on, better not to be attacked from both sides. I gave a course   as near as safely possible along the English coast.

We were given orders to land at Plymouth airport. We flew high enough to avoid the barrage balloons and at some point I instinctively told the pilot to dive below the clouds. We came down a few meters from one of the balloons. Sheer luck, not genius! Even the radar operator didn't see the balloons.

Plymouth airport was an American base and we were able to enjoy the facilities there. The food and the choice of food was unbelievable. We were always somewhat envious of the Americans, thanks to their high salaries, they had an advantage with girls. Never knew they also had a better choice of food.

Realising we won't be able to take off for a few days, I took the opportunity to visit my parents who were holidaying in Sandown, on the Isle of Wight. I had a good few days relaxation till I was called we had permission to take off. Had an opportunity to participate at a short tennis tournament.

There was another aircraft from our squadron on the same mission. I inquired how that plane fared. The news was bad. They didn't make it. The whole crew perished. The navigator Honza Hornung was one of the eight Navigators who trained together for two years. The others were, Václav Czapek, Pavel Dřevěný, Jan Filip,

Ludvík Košek, Miloslav Manásek, Rudof Němeček, Karel Novotný, Václav Tarantík. All were buried at a Plymouth cemetery.

# Chapter 7: World War 2   Experience

For some weeks in the spring of 1944, there had been rumours that the Allies were finally about to invade mainland Europe. We guessed this was soon to become reality when we were told we were all CB, Confined to Barracks. The camp was completely closed no one was allowed out. Our squadron was told that when the time came, our job would be to prevent any enemy boats or U-boats approach the English Channel. We were still continuing with our normal operational flights, concentrating on the south-west coast of England, round the area of Land's End.

After one such flight, assuming we had a two days' rest, I decided to skip camp. To get a pass to leave camp was no problem. Kurt Berman could copy any signature. I had a new girlfriend in London, and I decided to go and visit her. Right after debriefing, as we returned from a long flight, without rest, started the eight hours train journey from Cornwall to London. First I went home. There I was greeted by a message from my friend navigator, Kurt Berman, to get in touch with him urgently. *You are flying tonight* he said.

*I can't possibly get back in time.*

*OK*, said Kurt, *I'll take your place. You fly with my crew tomorrow*. I felt terrible, but there was nothing I could do now. With no chance to even see my girlfriend, I rushed back to the railway station. I had never experienced the feeling of a head-ache. There is always a first time. This was it. More than the head-ache, I couldn't even think how I would feel if something were to happen to Kurt on this flight. Never been so happy to see my crew back.

A few nights later, we were woken, *a special mission*. told to *prepare to fly*. We took off at 1am of June 6, 1944, five hours before the first troops landed on the beaches of Normandy. In the operation room we saw a red line between England and France. The same area that we had flown lately, between the coast of Cornwall and France. We suspected the red line to mean the invasion path but did not suspect the invasion would actually start, whilst we were in the air. We were to attack any suspicious object.

Never seen such a multitude of aircraft. We were flying low-level, above us Beaufighters, much higher *Matchsticks* as we called the Mosquito, made in Canada of wood. Possibly the most successful plane of WW2. Fighters were there high up to pounce on any enemy bombers or fighters trying to reach the invasion area.

Hard to describe the chaos, the disorder in the air on that first day of the invasion. The Germans had put booby-trapped objects in the sea. From a height they looked like boats. We flew at only 50 feet above the water, had to be careful not to be blown up with the object we attack. Two or more aircraft would go for the same target. Unbelievable what went on. Not a single enemy plane. How could they dare! The amazing thing was that we didn't realize at first that we were part of the invasion, we were too far west. As we got back to base, the invasion was already in full swing. The whole squadron was out to meet us, wanted to know what we saw. Our only answer *we saw aircraft, lots of aircraft*. We were the first crew to return this invasion day to our base.

By the second day, things seemed to be more organized. We now only had one free day between flights. We did more flights, but they were shorter.

We stayed in Cornwall another few months, then to Tain, on the east coast of Scotland, two hours by train north of Inverness. In the northern part of the Scottish highland. A naval base, also near us.

This transfer to the Scottish east coast because, after the invasion, the U-boats could no longer use the Bay of Biscay to get out into the open Atlantic. Our targets were now fjords on the vast coast of Norway and the Baltic Sea. This was now the only way for a U-boat to reach the vast Atlantic. The German Navy had a navigational aid operating in that area called *consuls*. The British Bletchley Park boys were great. They soon broke the German code, and we found these very useful. We still had to be on the alert because the Germans often found out we were locked on to their consuls and changed the frequency.

On a mission to one of the fjords, we saw a group of MTBs, motor torpedo boats. These boats were very fast and had no air defence. As we came nearer, their flags looked like Nazi ones. Though aware of the fact that the Norwegian flags were similar, we nevertheless went in to attack. I kept on repeating the colour of the flare identifying friendly boats. They were sure to fire a flare to identify themselves. Even enemy boats would fire a flare hoping to confuse the attacker. That is why I kept on repeating the colour, the gunners should not be fooled. The correct flare came up. The pilot swung the wings up and down, wishing them good luck. These Norwegians were real dare devils. They made lightning surprise landings, prearranged with the underground, causing the Germans a lot of trouble. We met the group again on their way back to England.

Our major operation we participated in was to the Baltic sea, November 1944. Our target the Danish island of Bornholm, which housed the biggest U-boat training school. We flew through the Skagerrak into Sweden and then down the west coast to Bornholm. The attack continued with relentless ferocity for three nights. Our crew took part in the attack only twice. About 1,200 aircraft took off. We had to keep strictly to our flight path. To deviate, would have meant interfering with another plane. The distance between each aircraft was half a minute on each side and half a minute ahead and aft. Just to imagine the noise of over a thousand planes flying over Sweden at night at rooftop level!

To our amazement, as we crossed the coast of Sweden near Halmstadt, we drew fire from Swedish coastal batteries. According to Intelligence reports, the Swedes never fired at German planes. Sweden altogether was co-operating with Nazi Germany. The war brought them much wealth.

Before the attack on Bornholm, we were sent from Tain to an airport between Londonderry and Colerain in Northern Ireland. We trained to fly with a special light, invented by a high RAF officer, named Leigh.

The Leigh light was a big monstrosity fixed to the side of one wing. That was problem number one. The pilot had to cope with an additional weight not evenly distributed. The light aimed downwards was idiocy number two. This gave the pilot the impression the plane is diving.

The idea, such a strong light aimed straight onto the U-boat would blind the crew. Good theory. What we and all other crews training with us realized, it is impossible to aim the light accurately at such a small target as a U-boat. We trained for three weeks, together with other squadrons. When the light was switched on, the pilot had

to close his eyes to avoid   him to pull up. We heard
of fatal mishaps by crews training before us. Loss of life
means very little to top commanders.

For the first Baltic attack, we used this Leigh light. As we
approached Bornholm, the radar operator spotted a target
and directed the pilot by *left–left, right-right* to it. *Over
target* the radar operator shouted and I switched on the
ingenious contraption. The light shone down into the
darkness and all we saw was darkness, but everybody on
the ground saw us. The whole world opened fire at us.
Never switched off a light that fast. All other crews
shared our experience. This time our protest worked. The
Leigh lights were removed.

What galls me to this very day is the waste of money
spent on all that training, and the guys who died during
those training flights. There wasn't one crew that thought
this could work. Back from that fancy training course, we
said this to our squadron leader. There was nothing he
could do, orders came from far higher up.

We were hit, but continued on our mission as Lada, the
flight mechanic, found nothing malfunctioning. We
succeeded to sink a U-boat. Ludek, first pilot, got a DFC
and I a DFM (RAF decorations) for this mission. (DFC
was for officers, DFM for NCOs).

Next night, out, to the Baltic again, same number of
aircraft, same targets. One difference, no Leigh Light to

burden the wing and burden us. Another, even more dangerous difference, the Germans were waiting for us. Didn't receive us kindly. Concentrated fire from all sides. Our aircraft was hit, probably badly, judging by the jolt it gave the plane. What damage, we didn't know. It was on the lower part of the aircraft. Lada said we have an oil leak. The question if the landing gear could be lowered pneumatically even if the landing gear was not hit. The debate, if to land in Sweden, a few minutes flying time. It would have meant the end of war for us. We knew the arrangement there. With a word of honour not to try to escape, British Airmen were free, could study at RAF expense.

Ludek (first pilot), Lada (flight mechanic), and myself put our heads together to consider the possibilities. Lada estimated the oil leak will not prevent us to fly another five hours with an economic use of the engines. I added that five hours is enough for us to reach Tain. The three of us realized the danger of flying with a damaged aircraft. At the same time we were aware of the fact that we may have to crash land. From Intelligence reports we knew that the Liberator would break into half, due to its empty middle section. In any sort of trouble after a crash landing we could definitely expect better assistance in England than in Sweden. Ludek now had to decide. His decision *we are going home.*

As we approached Sweden, Lada reported that we had still one bomb in the bomb rack. Shouted at the radar operator to find us a target. He found one. After jettisoning the bomb I realized we had hit a Swedish lighthouse. I recorded it in the log book, but the RAF claimed a German plane had bombed it.

First obstacle, the Swedes opened fire at us. We just went around the Swedish position far enough to be out of range. At about 200 kms. from Tain we switched on IFF and informed our home base we are coming in. Also informed them we may have to crash land as our landing gear may not function. Our base suggested to land in Stornoway. This is on the Isle of Lewis, part of the Hebrides Islands on the west coast of Scotland. We argued we cannot overfly Scotland, as climbing over the mountains would waste too much petrol and not enough to go all the way around Scotland. Our reasoning did not convince them. It was more important not to damage the airport. Like a doctor tells a patient it's too late to operate. Did they already decide we have no chance? The crew's spirit was at its lowest. We are being abandoned! With no other option we turned north to start the flight to reach the west side of Scotland . Still on the east side, we had to pass the most northerly RAF airbase, Wick. We tried our luck to let us land, maybe crash-land there. Not granted. No choice but try to reach Stornoway.

Limping along the coast of Scotland, reached the west side and not very far from the Isle of Lewis the aircraft started losing height. We threw out everything possible to lose weight, including our parachutes. They had no value. We were flying much too low anyway. Lada switched off the outer engines to save petrol. That must have done it. The aircraft levelled out at about 200 ft. No need to show our swimming ability in icy water! My position was in the fore part of the aircraft. I crawled back, handed the radio operator my note with our present position. *First send out a few times the distress signal SOS. As all go off the air, transmit our position.* His nerves gave. Sat stiff. Honza Gregor took over. Honza was excellent, most reliable at the radio and at the radar. Listening to the radio during a flight under normal circumstances felt like all the world sending messages at the same time. After our S.O.S. complete silence. Honza said like in the cemetery. Locked the radio on permanent transmission for others to get a bearing on us. Perhaps nearby boats can help in case we have to ditch. We fired all red rockets we had, for everyone in our vicinity to see that we are in distress. It was already dark.

I placed myself behind the pilots, to give visual instruction. Now only good nerves. Volka, the second pilot shouted to Ludek to turn east to mainland Scotland. It was very near and lovely rocks to crash into. Ludek did not even answer, he kept the course I gave him. The way to Stornoway was complicated. The runways were practically at sea level (good for us) but at the end of Broad Bay, not in a straight line. In other words visible when practically on it. I knew the base well. Landed there a number of times during navigation training.

Control tower asked us not to land on the runway, but parallel to it. It was in the direction of our approach. Ludek tried to lower the landing gear pneumatically. As correctly suspected, it did not work. Lada now tried to lower the landing gear manually without success. No luck.

Ludek's landing was dream-like. How lucky ! The ground was soft, entered the aircraft and lifted the main deck, where we all sat. Except the pilots, we were on the floor sitting against the flight direction with our heads down, firmly held by our hands. The impact with the ground was thunderous. I never believed in that split moment we could survive. Then another even more terrifying bang. Thought the plane was about to overturn. Then absolute quiet. I touched every part of my body, no pain. It took seconds to realize we made it. The plane did not break. No time to think. Had to get out before a fire or explosion. One by one we lifted ourselves through the emergency escape hatch, slid down the wing and jumped. Not a high jump, the wing was very near the ground. We were alive. We didn't know Lada had no time to come forward. He stayed in the least safe aft part, but made it. The only noise; from fire-engines and ambulances. They were there before we could    get out. They took us to the base clinic for a thorough check-up. We were all well. Probably twenty years older!

Our aircraft never caught fire nor did it explode, we had no petrol. Also the soft ground helped a lot. We were driven to the dining room and had a good meal served. Before we finished, our squadron leader flew in with a B24 to pick us up. He was a real daredevil type and that's how he flew the plane. Not what we needed just then. Still we reached Tain in one piece. Though late at night the whole squadron, ground and flying personnel, was out to give us a rousing welcome. Then again medical check-ups and again food. Still no chance to go to sleep. We had to give our side of the story; for an investigation. The main topic, why the flight engineer failed to get the wheels down. Did he forget to remove the safety pin or was it damaged ?

The third Baltic attack went without us. We were given a fortnight's leave, then returned to Tain. Only Gregor and myself continued operational flying. I joined the crew lead by Jan Riha.

From that time, November 1944, until the end of the war, I continued flying with my new crew.

There was no doubt December 31 1944 would be the last New Year's Eve of the war. Reason to rejoice ? No chance for three of our crews! Three aircrafts were required for a mission in the extreme north of Norway. The mission to destroy a U-boat, that was stuck in shallow water in one of the most northern fjords. The Germans were waiting for high tide. Jiři Osolsobě wrote in his book *Zbylo nas devět;* the most experienced crews were chosen. The navigators of these crews were, Mandler, Klemens and myself. The three of us did our training together. We were fitted with missiles, four on each side of the wing. We took off after midnight. During briefing we were told to expect that the U-boat crew will decide to escape in life boats. *Machine gun the lifeboats. The Germans can't survive the icy water.*

Our course was to go north to the Orkney Islands, our last pinpoint before aiming for Norway. We started in terrible weather. The meteorologist warned us to expect gale-force winds at some later stage. He must have known, he is not telling the truth. He just didn't want to frighten us. Right from the start a ferocious gale-force wind. We flew in low clouds with minimum visibility. Mandler's crew was first, then came Klemens , then us. After a couple of hours I realized we had been blown way off course, and I had no idea how far. By calculating the wind speed by the eddies, I found the wind was blowing at more than 100 miles an hour. I gave the pilot direction due east towards Norway. At least then we would get a pinpoint once we see the coast.

We reached Bergen. No   ac-ac fired at us. We could
see fighter planes on the ground. None took off. I did
reckon, we'll get no opposition in that storm. The
Germans were grounded, **we had to fly!** At least I now
knew where we were, could calculate the wind strength
and wind direction more accurately and set correct course
to reach the target. At this stage we did not know yet that
the first aircraft, with navigator Otto Mandler crashed on
one of the Orkney Islands – straight into a mountainside.

We carried on in the filthiest weather to the uppermost
part of Norway, near the Arctic Circle. Nearing the target
area we spotted the second Liberator leaving,
accompanied by fierce anti-aircraft fire. The U-boat was
already listing to one side. We went in for two
consecutive attacks to finish it off with our eight rockets.
The U-boat crew, in life-boats, had covered half the
distance to the coast. Our third attack was with machinegun fire attacking the lifeboats. We were low enough to
see the sailors jump into the water to save themselves.

We had reached our target area earlier than anticipated,
thanks to the strong tail wind on the outward flight. But
now we had the same strong gale blowing against us. The
weather did not get any better. I didn't want to
completely rely on the German Consul system. When I
saw a break in the clouds I managed to take a baring from
some stars. Though I had established that my average
error with the sextant was about thirty miles, taking the

appalling           weather   conditions into account, I based my calculations on a fifty mile error. I decided on an imaginary pin-point and gave the pilot a new, more southerly course, to be sure to hit land south of our base. As we reached the coast of the British Isles, turned north and landed in Tain dead on time.

As news came that the battleship Tirpitz, sister ship to the Bismarck broke out of a fjord, to the open sea, we were assigned to find her. Conducted a box formation search, when planes fly in overlapping allotted boxes. We knew it could break through somewhere between the Shetlands and Iceland. The obvious escape route. The ship couldn't in fact get out to the open sea but crept up to another fjord north of Tramso. She was eventually destroyed by a raid of 29 Lancaster bombers.

I always had a very academic interest in my navigational skills and often had long discussions with other navigators, and the Intelligence people. I was also very friendly with the navy navigators in our area. I noticed there was a very strong deviation of the magnetic compass on their naval maps near the area we were about to reach. A thought occurred to me and I asked whether there could be a similar effect at height. *How on earth should we know? We are always at sea, not in the air!* Came the reply.

The search for the Tirpitz gave me a chance to check if there is a different deviation than marked. I made various checks with the radio and sextant. Using maps, stars and planets, I realized we were far off course. We always strayed off course when flying in the western direction. I measured a deviation of nearly 20 degrees, by flying back east to the position we left.

Returning from the mission, another aircraft was about to start on the same task. I told Klemens, the navigator of that crew, about my findings.

When Klemens returned, he confirmed that I was right. We wrote a report to the Royal Geographical Association, and we both received a citation for that discovery.

Bad weather, which is 90% of the time in England, often affected us. On one of my leaves I hitched a lift with an English crew flying down to London. The weather was very stormy. One of the crew members approached me. We knew each other. *Can you help us? We are lost.* That was a good start to my holiday. The navigator was fairly new and had navigated way off course because of the bad weather. As there were thick clouds, we couldn't see any land below. It was certainly in my interest as well, to get to London safely. So instead of relaxing, I navigated the aircraft to its destination.

On another occasion, while returning from a patrol, we were hit by lightning. When that happens, all instruments are out. I just stood behind the pilot for the rest of the journey and navigated with   my thumb. Lucky it was after I gave the final course for the home base.

The war was nearing its end, Politicians were already manoeuvring themselves into position for post-war Europe.

In 1944, the Russians freed the eastern part of Czechoslovakia and set up a provisional government in Košice, the second biggest town in Slovakia. Slovakia, independent since March 1939, was governed by a Nazi priest, Tiso. The Slovaks had their own air force which fought on the German side. At a certain stage, except of one leading officer, the whole Slovak Air Force defected. Went over to the Russians.

The whole leadership of the Czech army and Air Force was strongly right wing. It was no secret that I was on the far left. Wherever I was together with Lada Novak we organized discussion groups. That was the case in St Athens, in the Bahamas and from day one when we joined the 311 squadron. The contact with our commander, Kostohryz was very cold.

Beneš, Czechoslovakia's president before Munich, joined the Košice government, which was mostly left-leaning. From then on our commander's attitude towards Lada and me became very friendly. Even called us to hear our view on present events.

Finally, this horrid war came to a close. When VE day finally came, we were all absolutely euphoric. Much less though, as the full horrors of the Nazi rule were revealed.

We were still attached to the RAF and our squadron was sent to the air base Manston in Kent, on the southeast coast of England near Ramsgate. The base had been used for fighters during the war. Fighters take off parallel to each other, six at a time, thus the runway was very wide, something we were not used to. Coming in the first time the pilot did not realize he has to land at the edge of the runway, misjudged the height and came down with a bang!

We were assigned to transport Czech nationals back to Prague, as ours was the only Czech bomber squadron with enough space to accommodate passengers, though not very comfortably. Most of them were Jews who had managed to escape to England before the war. Now, they wanted to return home to search for their loved ones. There were no passenger planes yet. The flight to Prague took three and a half hours, and we landed at Ruzyn airport. That airport is still used today, and it is amazing how it had been modernised. Back in 1945, it was still as primitive as pre-war.

I had very mixed feelings as we landed on Czech soil for the first time in six years. I had left as a young, inexperienced boy of 17. I was returning as a mature young man, who had faced danger and death many times. The first thing we did was to have a good meal in a Czech restaurant. I had never been a beer drinker. I had forgotten the Czech tradition, or I was too young before I left, to participate in it.

The first thing we were served without being asked, a mug of beer on a cardboard coaster. The waiter made a pencil mark on the coaster to indicate one beer. I decided to dispose of the beer as quickly as possible. Mistake ! The mug had hardly left my mouth, when a replacement was put in front of me, and another mark on the coaster. The waiter did not expect a non-drinker. That apparently did not exist in Czechoslovakia! Something else unusual, they placed an electric wand in the beer to warm it. Not refrigerated as today. Another tradition I had forgotten or rather had been too young to know about, was that tea was served with rum. I didn't like it. Drank for several years good strong English tea with milk! For Czechs, tea without rum is just not tea.

There was no supervision, no checking, no customs when we returned to England. I think I could have smuggled in the whole of Czechoslovakia. Unchallenged I brought my parents an original Czech porcelain dinner set. We had many requests to bring things from England. The most valuable items were flints for cigarette lighters and cigarettes.

We didn't have much time   for shopping as we either returned within a few hours or early the next morning. Our accommodation in Prague was at the Palace Hotel, today one of the top hotels in the city.

It was now that I started to hear stories about concentration camps. With hindsight it seems amazing that despite the fact that during the war I considered myself to be 'au fait' with everything around me, we had absolutely no conception what was really happening in Europe. Now we know, western leaders knew about it all along but kept it out of the news. They had to. How else hide the fact that they did absolutely **nothing** !

News came from the Russians, who were near the Polish border in the summer of 1944, that they see columns of smoke, and expressed their suspicion, people were being burnt. The reaction in the British press and radio; *Communist propaganda*. We now know, they knew it was true, but fooled the public. Anything distasteful was Communist propaganda.

During that summer of 1945 in Prague, survivors started trickling back. Their experience was difficult to grasp. These survivors were thankful to be alive. They were in too much shock to transmit or even to comprehend the enormity of the Nazi horrors they went through.

Survivors sought out the Jewish kapos, and members of the Judenrat from the ghettos. Many they killed. The

Judenrat officials had been willing or unwilling collaborators with the Nazis. They probably felt they would save their own skin. Shirer said in his book **The Rise and Fall of the Third Reich** that *if the Judenrat had not complied so easily, many lives would have been saved.* The Jews trusted the heads of the Judenrat. The Germans selected leading personalities. The Jews believed them, when told they will be interned or put to work. Obediently they assembled in specified places for deportation at the named hour. Had the Judenrat members spread the truth, most or many would have dispersed, escaped. The Germans did not have enough manpower to chase after them all. No wonder, after the war, concentration camp survivors were out to kill them. There were not many left anyway; most had been killed by the Germans. Others, when ordered to be on the council, committed suicide.

In September 1945 our squadron was officially transferred to the Czech Air Force. The first problem we faced was that of our rank. I was a flying officer – equivalent to a first lieutenant. My friends received one rank higher. The reason they had matriculated in Czechoslovakia, meaning before the war. I was too young for that. I matriculated in England during the war. To get the same rank I would have to complete my matriculation. To pass in Czech grammar and composition. Not a problem. But Czech literature was a different story. Too time consuming. A lot of reading. Didn't even try.

I hadn't considered what I wanted to do after the war. Before we all dispersed, representatives of foreign airlines, mainly South American, some European ones visited the squadrons looking for crews. I felt too politically involved in my country to go off somewhere else.

## Chapter 8: Return to Czechoslovakia

We accepted the new no-opposition system. All a result of the pre-war democracies' impotence to stop Hitler. We were inexperienced kids who had fought to establish a better, more just system. We detested the system of the Western democracies, who had sold Spain, Austria and our country. Czechoslovakia's democracy failed us. The government gave in to the West's betrayal, whilst the people were ready to fight. Today we know it could have prevented the war, more likely for Hitler to be overthrown.

The most senior Czech communist in England was Václav Nosek, who became the first Minister of Interior in post-war Czechoslovakia. Him and the one responsible for party members of the armed forces, Bedřich Hájek, I got to know through Lada Novak, my closest war time and post war friend. For us to be accepted to become members of the Communist party, we needed two sponsors. One was Nosek, the second was the head of the Prague party, who we didn't even know. Next was our acceptance to the Cadre department. The trusted circle of the party. Bedřich Hájek was there. The head was Jarmila Tausigová.

At the Communist party headquarter, an attractive building, a bank, next to the Brašná Brána (now again a bank) we were introduced to the head of the Armed Forces and Police department, František Vodička.

Vodička was a member of parliament at the pre-war parliament. His deputy, a young man, probably ten years older than myself, Josef Baudyš. Vodička was one of the old school, staunch Stalin supporter. Baudyš was very special. During the war, he was a steward on international trains criss-crossing Europe. A perfect occupation for passing messages for the underground. He made good use of this opportunity. He was a happy type, always smiling. With him I could discuss everything freely, also valued his opinion.

Soon after our transfer to the Czech Air Force, a crash course for education officers was organized. Both Lada and myself were asked to participate. It was an all-day three weeks' affair. From six in the morning until six p.m. We all probably only heard half of the lectures as by the afternoon we were half asleep. One of our lecturers was Vojtěch Kohout, a Russian major. He did speak Czech fairly well with a strong Russian accent. To prove his Czech ancestry, he claimed that three generations ago his family came from Jihlava in eastern Bohemia. It wasn't difficult to discover he was a Russian, not Czech patriot.

At the end of the course, I was posted as education officer to the air force base near Liberec. I stayed at the hotel *Zlata Husa,* number one hotel even today. The 1,100 or so airmen at the camp, were aircraft mechanics, who had worked in German factories or German airbases during the war. The advantage, these boys required minimum training before getting posted to Airports all over the country.

Liberec, or German, Reichenberg, was the biggest town in the Sudeten area, all German. The German population was still there. They were made to have a yellow band on the sleeve of the outer garment. A taste what the Jews felt with the same armbands. Here is the big difference. No-one bothered them, beat them nor took pot shots at them for fun. During the initial unsettled period, the first few months after the end of the war, rumours circulated about armed groups. Assumed marauding German ex-soldiers, stealing, terrorizing the local population. We had reports of attacks against villages in the nearby mountainous areas near the border. Germans were still living there as in the whole Sudeten area, before being expelled to Germany.

I decided to find out who these bandits really are. I asked for 60 volunteers for this action. We crept up to the border at night and lay in wait. The first night, all was quiet. Just one incident. There was a general night curfew. I was called as a number of my boys held a German who was caught outside. He was all trembling. I asked him in German what he was doing outside. He explained he only wanted to go to the toilet which is outside. I told him not to be afraid, our soldiers don't behave the way the Germans did. He went back to his house. With the case closed my soldiers were enraged why I spoke to him so humanly and in German. *Do you know how the Germans behaved ?* Yes I knew, not on my own skin, but I knew. At that moment I realized what beasts the Germans were. How can I beat an unarmed man, kick him or even just shout at a defenceless individual. With the Germans this didn't count, even if this were a woman or just a child. I went to a German school, I had many German friends. Those same friends with an upbringing like mine, did they become subhuman !?

The next night the boys went without me. They came to my room at the hotel but did not succeed to wake me.

The third night we caught the thieves. Not Germans, a unit of Russian soldiers lead by an officer, going out on a looting spree.

I jumped from my hiding place and confronted their officer without taking my revolver out of the holster. As the Russians cocked their rifles, my boys came out of the bushes from both sides of the road with guns pointing at them. The Russians didn't try anything. We called the police, who came and took them away in a truck. Probably 20 of them. Later I asked a police officer what they did with the Russian thieves. *Handed them over to their units.* It transpired that these Russian soldiers were selling the stolen goods to dealers in town, who had their clients in Prague and other    places. The dealers were arrested.

The officers of the base had their offices in separate billets. The commander, a major of the old school. A lieutenant was in charge of military training. He was in command of the non-commissioned officers, all Slovaks, who trained the boys. Why Slovak instructors? Slovakia had an army during the war, under the Germans. Czechs did not. I didn't like their brutal inconsiderate methods, they learned from the Germans. I was told of unacceptable excesses. Together with their commanding officer we assembled all non-commissioned officers. I gave them a severe dressing down, their commanding officer continued with practical hints how it is proper to act severally, yet humanly.

There was another education officer on the base, a captain, probably in the forties. Though I often met him at officers' meetings, never understood his function.

I, much younger and lower in rank was deputy commander.

Every morning all men assembled for physical exercise, then technical training. I encouraged discussion groups formed in each hut of about 50 men. To find out the boys' political preferences I came up with the idea of organizing elections. It had to be prepared in such a way that the actual elections; placing a ballot box, in each hut, the voting, collecting the ballot boxes and counting the votes be done at utmost speed. I did not imagine the Camp Commander would not get to know about it. But he should find out, after it was all over. I planned carefully. Asked two airmen from each billet to prepare the ballot boxes and slips of paper with all four political parties. All being ready, one evening the boys placed the ballot boxes in each hut and asked the airmen to place their vote. It all happened very quickly. In each billet the boxes were then opened and the slips counted openly, for everyone to see, thus assuring the counting was correct. The same evening I had a list of how each hut voted.

It suddenly dawned on me, what I did so efficiently could put me in a lot of trouble. It after all was a political act not really acceptable in the Armed Forces. I wanted to be sure I can get some backing from higher up. I went to Prague and spoke to Imrich Rot. Within the army's education department, he headed the political section. He had served in the Czechoslovak army in Russia and was a close friend of Bedřich Rajcin, head of Intelligence, later also deputy Minister of Defence.

Imrich Rot, by profession an engineer, very sharp mind. He asked me a lot of questions. I handed him the paper with the election results. He never decided on the spot, always took some time to weigh the problem before answering. I went to the near-by Broadway passage for a coffee and horké párky and   back to Imrich. The answer was, I don't need to worry.

I understand Imrich Rot was killed in a car accident in 1951, driving his own car. Accident ?

In Liberec I was at an officers' meeting when the forthcoming marriage of one of the officers was being discussed. The officer in question was not permitted to participate. Apparently he had to give the commanding officer all details of his bride-to-be and her family and ask for consent to marry her. I was stun at the whole procedure and at the details discussed. I was speechless.

I attended a few social events organized by the municipality. Befriended the daughter of one of the local officials, who later came to visit me in Prague. She was too serious and I too young to think of a permanent bond.

I was asked to participate at a meeting of education officers in Hradec Králové. When the hotel clerk at the check-in desk mentioned my room number, an attractive young lady standing next to me said: that's next to my room. I didn't take much notice. When in the middle of the night I opened my door, hearing a knock, it was the same young lady or not lady. I should have suspected it could be a plant, but didn't. Enjoyed a good time. A couple of days after the Hradec Králové conference, my commanding officer asked me to come to his office. He showed me a photo of that same woman in my Liberec hotel room wearing my uniform including my cap. I didn't understand what he wanted to prove and anyway how she got the key to enter my room. Without someone important she could definitively not get my room key, even less to have her picture taken. What I did understand, the Major must have had a hand in this or even initiated the whole affair. I went to Prague for a few days. I told Kohout and Yosef Baudyš about this episode. Back in Liberec the Commanding Officer came to my office. Very unusual. He had never come to my office before. What he came to discuss, he could have called me to come to his office. He was unusually friendly. Was that an apology? Did someone express displeasure for his little trick he played on me ? I can imagine he was not happy to have such a young deputy.

My pleasant stay in Liberec came to an abrupt end. Major Vojtěch Kohout, the same person who was lecturing at the crash course for education officers, came to see me in Liberec. Major Kohout then was head of the Department of Education at the Air Force General Staff Headquarters, as such, deputy to the Chief of Staff of the Air Force. The Department of Education was in fact the all-powerful political department. Kohout asked me to come to Prague to become his deputy.

On Jan 1, 1946 I reported at my new assignment which was in the building of the Ministry of Defence in Dejvice.

At the Air Force Headquarters there were not many who had fought during the war. Those that did, like Kohout and myself, were looked on with more respect. The majority of the officers, who survived the war at home were commonly called *mothball officers*. The Air Force Headquarters occupied one floor of the Ministry. I now had easy access to other departments of the ministry. I was very mobile. I had a car at my disposal, a Wanderer, a German army car, still with a Wehrmacht insignia. Official cars were not driven by officers but professional drivers only. My driver was great. From him I learned a lot what it was like to live under German occupation.

I had to visit all the bases and keep myself up to date with all the goings on at every base. If the base wasn't too far away I went in my official car if the base was further afield I went by train or plane, a German Fieseler-Storch. My purpose, to get acquainted with the commanders, officers and discuss the activities of the Education Officers. I knew every airport and every air base in the Czech countries.

This brought me to Havlíčkův Brod. German airmen were interned there. My first chance to speak to the opposite side. They were glad to have someone to speak to them in German. I asked, what they thought how the war would end. These were boys, who were not in the Luftwaffe from the beginning. What they experienced was retreat after retreat. Their only dream to be back at home. They were absolutely stunned, when I told them I am Jewish. I visited them a number of times. On one occasion, they gave me a huge painting of Stalin, painted by one of them. I was told, a present from the whole group. I had no idea how they got the very fancy frame. I hung it up in the living room. Not very appreciated by the US Embassy staff, who rented my apartment later.

With Kohout, my boss, I got along well. He travelled very often to Moscow. Though, where ever I went he got a full report, I had no idea what his visits were for. Once he returned with a young Russian Air Force officer. Three years older than I. A fighter pilot with many operational hours to his credit. He brought seven Russian victory medals. One I got. Who deserves the other six, Kohout asked me to choose. I already had a few medals. The ones having a meaning, two for VALOR, for each 200 operational hours, one MILITARY CROSS for 500 operational hours, one English medal DFM for sinking a U-boat. The only one I really value, that I stayed alive.

I spent many hours with the Russian pilot. He was sure the Soviet regime will be much more liberal, as the population proved their patriotism. During the war it did seem going that way. How disappointing it must have been for people like him, when the terror resumed again.

The first disagreement with Kohout, when General Plass, in charge of pilot training, was selected to be Military Attaché in London. Our department also had to approve his assignment. I said *over my dead body*, Kohout signed behind my back.

My contacts were much closer and more frequent with Imrich Rot, head of the Army's political department. Also useful to exchange speeches for high officers and dignitaries attending festive openings of memorial statues.

Being at General Staff headquarters gave me access to a variety of classified information. Every paper we received, we had to sign for. Then gave it a number in our register with the date received and the date forwarded. When not interested to forward it, I just left it in the drawer. It took weeks before someone woke up to look for it and trace where it got stuck. Sometimes nobody bothered.

Europe in those days was one big displaced persons' camp. Once survivors had regained some strength they returned to their home towns to search for other members of their families and friends. Most of our family who remained behind were killed. My uncle who had built the big carton factory, had emigrated to Palestine in the thirties, but was on a family visit in Europe, when the war broke out. We never heard from him again. My father's brother, who lived in Paris fought with the

Maquis. He was caught together with his wife a couple of days before Paris was liberated and executed. Their only son, Shimon, survived and married after the war a young woman, his partner in the underground. All this I didn't know, when December 1944 I joined a plane from our base going to Paris (Paris was liberated August 1944). I went to my uncle's pre-war address and found Shimon and his wife.

Couldn't see that Paris had gone through a brutal war. Lights on, night clubs active as if nothing had happened. My cousin took me to Folly's Berger, to good restaurants, also to a movie giving an American film, so I could understand. I didn't, it was dubbed. The evening I was to fly back, the flight was postponed for the next morning. With nothing to do, I went to a dinner dance. I still remembered my high school French. I asked a girl to dance with me, she refused and so did another one. I approached a table with many girls and boys. The girl I asked, again refused. A boy at the table nudged her to dance. An opportunity to find out what is wrong with me. Never expected the answer she gave. *We hate the British.* I had come in my battle dress. Only on the gala tunic's shoulders Czechoslovakia appeared. I stopped, showed her my Air Force identity card. It had Czechoslovakia written in big letters. A sudden transformation from her stern look to a hearty smile. She ran over to her friends to show my card. Now I was a welcome guest at their table. The reason, they expected to be liberated at least three years earlier. Repeating De Gaulle's critic. He was their hero. The Allies never informed De Gaulle of their intention of operation Torch. They couldn't. They concocted it with the pro-Nazi French leaders.

Father's six sisters and their families all perished. except one of his nieces. A few years after the war we received a letter from her from Kazakhstan.

From my mother's side, one of her sisters came to Palestine in 1925 with husband and five kids. The sixth, Ben-Ami, was born Palestine. The first born child in Magdiel. A brother lived in Leipzig and moved with his wife to Palestine in the thirties. A niece, Ryvka, came to Palestine in 1935, another Hana, arrived in Palestine the day WWII broke out. One of my mother's brothers came to Palestine with the 2nd Aliya. He apparently drowned whilst swimming. My mother's parents, 2 sisters, 2 brothers and their six children perished in the holocaust.

Lists started coming in of survivors from the concentration camps. I went through them thoroughly. Less than half a dozen of my friends were on the lists. I had no problem to locate them. Bochner, of all the possible jobs I could arrange, chose to join the police. I visited Teplice a number of times. Who I mostly met were those, who like myself, hoped to find friends or family. Two brothers Vječner survived. Unfortunately the older one overate like so many, after the years of starvation .He died soon after liberation. The younger one

I remembered as remarkably good at drawing at the age of 9. I got him to come to Prague. Gave him some contacts. Very quickly he acquired a well-paid job, drawing the big cinema displays. Did very well. I felt very proud of him. He kept in touch with me, as long as I was in Prague. Langerova, who joined my class in Duchcov in the third year, survived a concentration camp. Like all survivors I knew, I also visited her. The only one to give me a cold reception. Very abrupt negative reply, when I asked, if she needs any help.

I made a special visit to Zeleneč to search for my Czech parents. Father, not yet 50 years of age, had died of a liver illness. His many beers finished him. Mother was delighted to see I had survived and many of the village turned out to greet me.

I also helped people reclaim their property. And here we struck many awkward situations. The son of a Jewish farmer returned after serving in England. His father perished in a concentration camp. The farm was now owned by a Czech family. It wasn't an easy situation. With the help of the deputy to the Minister of Agriculture, Gaertner, who served with me in the same squadron, I succeeded to get him possession of the farm despite the opposition of the local council. At one of the hearings when I put forward my views in favour of the rightful owner, the local Communist Party head (council chairman) attacked me.

*Why are you defending a Jew? You're not Jewish.*

*As long as you're an anti-Semite, I'm a Jew*, was my answer.

In those days before instant communication, the Ministry of Defence had one single telex machine. It was in the basement and served the whole building. One day, I was told there was an urgent message for me. I took the paternoster, a constantly moving elevator. Had to jump in when it reached my level and jump out at destination. The education officer at the Sternberg Air Force base was at the other end at the telex. He asked me to come to see him as soon as possible.

The story I heard, that the heads of all four political parties at the municipality were squandering money on entertainment for themselves as if there was no limit. Not a good socialist example for the citizens! I returned to Prague and gave a report to the head of the Zemsky Narodni Vybor. Head of all municipalities. He investigated and soon I was informed all four councillors were sacked.

I was impressed. This then was the atmosphere in post-war Czechoslovakia. We had the feeling we are building a new country, clean and just. To a common goal: an honest type of socialism.

Lenhoff, one of the eight navigators who I trained together with, introduced me to an elderly German couple he knew from pre-war times. I understood he was friendly with their daughter, who now was married and about to leave for Germany. They were ready to let me a room in their very large apartment. It was very centrally located, on Karlovo Naměstí. Very elegant, old style furniture. My room had its own bathroom. The old people looked sad and frightened. Never saw a smile on their face. They had employed a local lawyer who tried not to have them deported to Germany. Had they been happier during the German occupation ? Maybe, they felt then on top of the world. I never discussed the past with them. Some evenings they invited me to have coffee with them. I was never there during the day. I listened to stories of the bad times during the occupation. I never argued. Living in such a rich home, they couldn't have had it so bad. When the time for their deportation came, their lawyer asked me if I could help in any way. Even if I could I wouldn't lift a finger.

A dress maker, who employed a number of young seamstresses was a floor below. I made myself popular, bringing them cigarettes from my numerous trips to England. With one of the young seamstresses I got more than friendly and spent a couple of week-ends at a hut she possessed on the banks of the Vltava.

I flew all around the country visiting my mechanics (from Liberec) at the various airport bases. However, all was not perfect. Working at headquarters, it did not take me long to observe the strong Russian influence that was beginning to take over.

I attended a lecture given by Dr.Stoll, professor at Karlova Universita. During question time, I raised my hand to challenge something he said. The subject was philosophical, *if something can happen by chance.* As I was the first and as it turned out the only one to place a question I was surprised to have to give my name and which branch of the communist party I belonged to. Not that it really worried me. I argued a point, and Dr Stoll convinced me that I was wrong. However, as I learned later, just queering Dr Stoll was not kosher.

The next day, Bedřich Hájek, of the cadre department of the communist party, summoned me to his office. This is the same Bedřich who I knew from England. Whilst in his office, Madame Taussigová, head of the cadres, came in and started shouting at me for daring to criticize Dr Stoll.

I was aghast. It was not even a political discussion. I didn't let it go. *We are not in Russia,* I yelled back.

Stunned, she did not reply and returned to her room. Though Taussigová was a staunch supporter of the Stalin type regime, it didn't help her when the top communist leadership was arrested in the early fifties, culminating in the Slánsky trial. That trial had a strong anti-Semitic connotation and Tausigová was Jewish, so was Hájek. Both got a 20 year sentence. They were released in 1963.

In April 1946, elections were held in Czechoslovakia. In the months prior to the election, I was involved in campaigning for the communist party and was an observer at the communist congress which preceded it.

Prior to the election campaign, the communist party asked the Russians to have their army leave the country. The leaders were justifiably afraid to lose the elections if there was still a Red Army presence.

It was at one of the pre-election parties, when foreign correspondents were also invited, that I met Eva Mudrova. She acted as an interpreter for one of the foreign guests. Extremely intelligent young lady, my age. I found a lovely companion. Accompanied me to parties, theatres, concerts, operas. We kept in touch after I left for England. During the Prague Spring she took a holiday in Europe, rang me from Geneve, that she got stuck without money, having prolonged her stay due to the Russian Army entering Prague. It was easy to help her, asked Aby, my brother-in-law, who happened to be in that town. She came to Israel, thought she could get all the advantages of a New Immigrant and ask her husband to join her. She was wrong. That privilege was only for

Jews. During my many Prague visits with Sally, after the fall of the Red Empire, Eva and Honza, her husband, were our constant companions.

# Chapter 9: Politics, Politics

Many people who read my story probably recall scenes from communist party congresses in the Soviet Union. Hundreds or thousands of delegates sitting in a great hall bedecked and festooned with the red flag of the workers and other communist symbols. Barely visible behind the podium is the speaker, speaking, speaking, speaking hour after hour after hour.

So it was with our congress at the Representační Dům. Not the huge Soviet venue, but hours and hours of speeches. I could never prove it, but somewhere in some communist officials handbook there must be a clause which states the higher your rank, the longer you speak. Slánský's speech must have lasted four hours at least.

My boss Kohout was furious that I had been selected and not he to be an observer at the congress. Officially, as members of the armed forces, we were not allowed to belong to a political party. The party invited observers from each of the forces.

Between the congress and the actual election, there were a couple of months for campaigning. I had to be careful; I held my 'political' meetings away from the bases, in the local towns, not public meetings, just speaking to small selected groups. My *line* was to promote our new brand of socialism, without dictatorship a la Russia. Some of the pre-war leaders were Stalin supporters. We were optimistic to succeed with    our line, encouraged by the West European, particularly the Italian party and the general atmosphere in post-war Europe, where socialists were gaining ground. Even Britain's prime minister Winston Churchill lost the first post-war elections to the British Labour party.

I was always in uniform and spoke to separate groups of soldiers and civilians. The civilian meetings were more public. Although I was treading on dangerous ground, I relied on the power of the communist party, as my protection. As I moved around the country, I occasionally came across people I knew, either from my childhood or from the war days. I always felt I was more convincing to these people, as all of us who had been actively serving during the war.

Forever trying to do something unique, I came up with the idea to have thousands of army and air force boys march through the streets of Prague in support of the communist party. I told my boss, Kohout. He liked the idea. Not knowing the Army units, I asked the Army political department for help. It was a great success. I never thought so many boys would want to participate. The right wing press the next day mentioned my name as the Moscow trained organizer. The only time I ever was in Moscow, was a few days in December 1940 on the way to Vladivostok.

I asked the Minister of Information, Václav Kopecky to speak to the officers at the Ministry of Defence. I regretted that choice as his theme turned out to be a threat *if you don't vote for the communist party* and so on. A real blind, pro Stalinist line. I paid him a visit at the Ministry later and told him he had probably lost us more votes than gain any. *I do hope you don't think we should have a dictatorial regime.* He just smiled. Probably knew more than me and smiled at my naivety

Just before the elections, there was a huge convention of all WW2 veterans. It was held at the same Representační Dům. A couple of weeks before the convention I was approached by the head of Army Intelligence. This is the first time I met Bedřich Rajcín. He introduced me to his deputy, štábní kapitán Vaš. Rajcín was then a major. Both had fought with the Czechoslovak Army in Russia. They wanted me to speak at the convention. Rajcín's deputy was to discuss with me the line I should take. He gave me general guidelines. Basically I had to attack the pre-war Western leadership that got us into the war. I reminded my listeners that we had all our experience of **their** kind of democracy. Now was the time for a new approach, a socialist country, but a new form of socialism, not like our neighbours farther east, but OUR way. This then was the communist motto *to socialism, our way*. (k socializmu, naší cestou).

When I thought of it later, to have all four parties in the government and no opposition, was dangerous. But we didn't see it that way in 1946. We felt we were in an emergency situation, and this was what was needed to rebuild the country. I still remembered how the world's great democracies had behaved prior to the second world war. I despised democracy, and could not see the importance of an opposition. The trauma of Munich burdened on us heavily.

When the elections results were announced, the communist party had won 38% of the vote, thus became the biggest political party. Gottwald became prime minister. In Slovakia there were only 2 parties and the communists lost. The Agrarian party won two thirds of the vote.

In Slovakia anti-Semitism was high, including within the communist party. The reason why Slovak Jewish communist leaders were transferred to the Czech countries.

After the elections, all the representation in the local government and local councils had to be re-shuffled according to the percentage of votes the parties achieved.

I was still travelling to and from England using my RAF Identity card. But eventually I would have to get a Czech passport. To obtain a passport, and therefore prove the Czech citizenship, one had to prove residency somewhere. Father' home town was Oldřichov (Ullersdorf). Now my name was a problem. At Air Force Headquarters, I asked not to revert to my original name, as my brother kept the new name as well. I was not requested to legalize the change, as my brother did in England. This I didn't know at the time. Didn't even think it is important. To avoid any problems, I contacted the head of the country's Head of municipalities to speak to the mayor of Oldřichov. Didn't have to. The mayor was my close friend and class mate at the Duchcov gymnasium. Added my new name to the previous one and gave me the document I needed in my new name only. The gymnasium director to certify that I visited a Czech school, wrote both names. Though he didn't know me, used the school photos to make sure. I stayed another day with Oldřich Bogner, the mayor (předseda narodního výboru). Talking about the war years. Another two days in Teplice, just to roam around. Very sad indeed. My home town, a strange city.

By now, things were heating up in the office; I had no time to pursue the passport. After the party congress, things became very strained between my boss, Kohout, and myself. We shared a room, which was fortunately huge.

The communist party chiefs were becoming more and more uneasy with Kohout's very frequent trips to Moscow. At Air Force headquarters meetings I attended in my boss' place. At one of these meetings I was asked where Kohout was. When I replied he was in Moscow, the next question, what he was doing there. *Perhaps he's gone for someone else* I impetuously replied, *certainly not for us.* You could have heard the proverbial pin drop. Everyone suspected him, but who would dare to say anything? I had spelled it out.

Kohout was full of tricks. One day he started *I'll get that Nazi.* He meant the Head of the Slovak Air Force. Slovakia was autonomous and the country had its own forces. This Chief of Staff held the same position during the German occupation. Kohout wanted to get rid of him. Wanted to prove that he was a Nazi sympathizer. During the war the Slovak Air Force Commander published a journal. Kohout thought that by going through all these publications we would find evidence of his pro-Nazi stance. This was a huge job, which he threw on my lap. Had to sift through dozens of publications and analyse every article, every sentence, every word.

I devised an efficient way to do this. I approached the political faculty of the university, where I was also studying and hired a number of students to go through the journals. I took on purpose known communists. There should be no suspicion of an attempt to white-wash the Slovak boss. After the students finished their work, I compiled a summary report. The conclusion was that this man was clean, even evidence that he had been anti-

German. When I handed over the final report to Kohout, I think he would have liked to kill me! My report was top secret, yet the more secret, the faster the news travel.

I was called to a secret meeting at Air Force Headquarters. There I was informed that the British and Americans were flying over Eastern Slovakia, dropping radios and arms to anti-government groups. It was not possible to send out an official written order to open fire, even shoot down Allied planes. I should pass on the order in person.

I was not very happy with the task I was given and decided to consult somebody. The obvious person was Beldřich Rajcín head of Army Intelligence. He was no longer a stranger to me, I had met him on various occasions, never to consult him on any subject. Though an ardent communist, he disliked the Russian system not less than myself. In this case, instead of answering my question, he gave me a long lecture about the art of disinformation. I understood perfectly what he meant and that he meant the Russians.

My first destination was Bratislava, by train, to see the Chief of the Slovak Air Force. The same person Kohout wanted to have removed. Although he didn't say anything to me directly, the way he received me, he obviously knew all about my report and my conclusions. Having only known me by name, he was surprised I am that young. He greeted me   as his best friend. On the subject I came for, he assured me there were no roaming gangs and no English nor American planes flying over Slovak territory. In Prague they are dreaming. I spent three fabulous days in Bratislava. I was taken to dinner parties, nightclubs, you name it. Instead of by train, I was provided with an airplane to take me to the next Air Force base, Tri Duby in Banska Bystrica. It must have been the Commander's work, that I was received royally on arrival. The Air Base commander and a number of officers were there to receive me. Specially sent by Air Force Headquarters from Prague, their faces showed surprise to see such a young officer. After all I was just 24 and always looked younger than my age. We soon got very friendly. I gave the commander the message I brought from Prague. Like in Bratislava, he assured me nothing of this sort is happening here. I thought of Rajcín's lecture. I ate and drank and listened to their war-time experience. Their defection to the Russian side.

My next visit was the Air Base in Spiská Nová Ves, the most eastern Air- Force base of Slovakia. I reached it by train. The reception there was less friendly. Nor was I, knowing that the commanding officer was the only pilot who did not defect to the Russians. The commander already knew what I came for. Without waiting for me to speak: *You are a naive young man. I can only fire at aircraft with insignia of an enemy country* . There was another matter I had to discuss with the same General.

The education officer in Bratislava told me of a sergeant being held in confinement for months for some political reason. I was allowed to see that sergeant. My conclusion that it was a personal vendetta. Not being a judge, I got in touch with the Commander in Bratislava and told him what this sergeant said. I was later informed that military police was sent to the Spiská Nová Ves base, took the sergeant to Bratislava and freed him.

Back in Prague I was presented with an expense account I was supposed to have incurred during my trip. All I had to do was to sign on the dotted line. This included first class hotel accommodation and expensive restaurant meals. First class train tickets and a generous daily allowance. No need to produce receipts. I told the accountant I didn't have any of these expenses. I slept at Air Force bases and never paid for a meal. This, I was told is **the procedure** and not to argue.

For the coming X-mas holidays I invited parents to spend with me in the Tatra mountains, in Slovakia. The day after they arrived a telegram came from London that Steffi gave birth. It was a boy and their first grandchild. Parents flew back to London. I took the Tatra holiday on my own. No skiing, there was no snow. The skiers were filling the lobbies. I was in uniform. From my last visit to London I brought 12 suit lengths, but didn't yet give them to a tailor. Good readymade suits were not yet the rule.

Though I had put the Czech rank on my tunic, it still was an obvious RAF uniform. From a young group one came over to invite me to join them. Very jolly youngsters. Thanks to them, despite the absence of snow I spent a pleasant holiday. The father of one of the boys was a General. This was General Píka. I heard of him, but never met him before. Back in Prague I was invited to a number of parties by the same group. General Píka was Czechoslovak's Military Attaché in Moscow till the end of the war. After the war Deputy Chief of the General Staff. Executed in 1949.

I understand that 50 per cent of all Czechoslovak soldiers in Russia were Jews. It may not have been the same proportion in the Czechoslovak Army in England and in the Czech squadrons of the RAF. Yet a high percentage. In the post-war leadership of the Communist Party the percentage of Jews was high as well. Anti-Semitic tendencies started showing themselves in the army leadership. Another phenomena, discrimination against soldiers having fought in the Spanish civil war. Láda Novák was one of them. He told me that the commanding officer of the Czechoslovak brigade in Spain, a Slovák was demoted to a low rank. We knew about the mistreatment of Russians who had fought in Spain, though in fact sent by their own government. I discussed this development with Lada and we decided to request a meeting with Rudolf Slánsky. Slánsky, as well as being secretary of the communist party, was the parliamentary secretary for Defense. We visited him in his parliament office, in that capacity. We didn't think he knew who we are. We decided, Lada to speak about discrimination against Jews and I about the Spanish fighters.

Slánsky did not agree with our assessment and refused to admit there is any discrimination. As he raised his voice, so did we and left his office, not as friends.

Slánsky surely must have known about all these happenings and must have known who is behind all this. If he didn't, we gave him names he could check.

Things started to happen that had no explanation.

I travelled to England fairly regularly to visit my parents. Father had set up a textile business since 1939 and Henry joined him. After one of these visits, I returned to my apartment in Prague late at night. Exhausted, I fell into a deep sleep.

My slumber was shattered by a loud banging on my door. Half asleep, I saw it was still the middle of the night. At the door were two military policemen from the air force, both from my squadron. I knew them well and I knew they were far from being communist friendly. What did they want? They had orders to search my apartment. They were looking for some incriminating evidence to prove that I was involved in some plot against the state. All was done in a friendly spirit. After all we were war time friends. They didn't stay very long but it was enough to make me think. To give people, opposed to the regime important security jobs, such people are loyal, as they don't expect to be treated well. The cunning Russian system. Genghis Khan used this method, or probably even someone before him.

I had good enough contacts to make waves. I went to my most trusted friends and complained bitterly. They found that it was my boss, Kohout, who had ordered the investigation.

It was not feasible now I should stay in the same office with Kohout. I moved to the Army's political department run by Imrich Rot. Brought all my files and continued the same work from his office.

I couldn't relax for long. An order came through that I was to be posted to Brno. Nobody in Czech headquarters knew anything about it. The order had come from somewhere else. Not finding the source of my demotion, which it was, compared to my position at the Air Force Headquarters in Prague, I told everyone concerned that I intend to resign. I requested a meeting with the Chief of Staff of the Air Force and told him of my decision. I had a call from Vodička, head of the Defence department in the Communist Party, as such Josef Baudys' boss. He was against me resigning. He offered me a promotion to the rank of major and to be sent to study at the Frunze

Military Academy in Moscow. I was just 25 and this was certainly a great push forward.

Yet Moscow was the last place I wanted to go to. The height of irony! *A committed communist is afraid to go to the heart of the socialist Motherland*! I was already then good in geography. I knew there is lots of space in Siberia. I then discussed the offer at Vodička's adjacent office with Josef Baudyš. With him I could speak frankly and told him about my reservations. Only a couple of days later I was given an alternative offer to become Military Attaché in China. I was under the impression that this is a serious offer as I was given a private tutor to teach me Chinese and a very elegant, elderly lady to teach me diplomatic etiquette. I studied intensively with both tutors for a few weeks and just as suddenly as these tutors appeared they stopped showing up. No explanation! Nothing! I decided there and then to leave the Air Force and go to London where my parents live. Number one I needed a passport and recommendations to permit me study abroad. I didn't want to just leave. It should be official with all the permits from the highest places. I flew to England to register at LSE, *London School of Economics.* Had to pass exams first and returned to Prague. I chose economics and international relations, as these were the subjects I already studied at the Prague University whilst serving. It didn't take long to be informed I passed my entrance exams.

Luck was on my side. Václav Kopecky, the Minister of Information called me to his office. We had met before the elections a year ago. He told me about an upcoming International Youth Festival to be held in Prague, that summer, 1947. As minister of Information, Kopecky was in charge of all the arrangements. He had originally given the task to students, only to discover they could not cope with such an undertaking. Seventeen thousand young people were expected from all over the world. Accommodation, transportation, food facilities, interpreters, entertainment, meetings, lectures, sight-seeing tours, all this had to be organized. He asked for four young officers to help out and I was one of those recommended. The minister wanted me to be in charge of interpreters. *The most important political job,* he said. My job was to supervise the interviewing of prospective candidates in all required languages, then placing them as required. I basically agreed. Then told the Minister about my intention to study in London. Taking this assignment will not give me time to go through all the red tape to get a passport. *I am sure, you, a Minister, can do it much faster and get my passport ready at the end of the festival.* Smilingly he agreed and we shook on it. Kopecky introduced me to two young men from his office, who were to assist me. The Air Force gave me leave to carry out this task.

And what a task it was. Oversee interviewing hundreds of students. Help assess the results and decide who is and who isn't fit for the job. I   had the two boys from the Kopecky's ministry to help me, plus two University students I chose to be always at my side and two students good at the languages we needed: English, French, Italian, German. German we needed for the Austrian delegation. Germans were not invited. The goal: 450 interpreters. The interviewing was in full swing when I came into the picture. This now, three weeks before the festival was to start.

As the delegations started to arrive. They had to be met at the railway station by interpreters of their language. The students in charge of accommodation had to be present to direct them to their living quarters. Transportation people had to be there. Schools were converted to hostels for the time of the festival.

Needless to say, there was no electronic equipment in those days, no cellular phones. I would get a call that a minister would be speaking in Czech, and interpreters for French, German, English, Italian were required. For such occasions I had a small group of the best interpreters capable of simultaneous translation. Surprisingly these were all girls, not a single boy. To follow events, arrangements, the unavoidable constant changes, we used the big school blackboards. The blackboard boys and girls were the busiest and most important for the organization to function.

Delegations were allocated rooms according to languages and assigned the relevant interpreters to each school. In my office, a very spacious room, probably the school conference room, were the heads of the departments. Also a few interpreters, who could go where necessary at short notice.

The three weeks of the festival I didn't sleep properly. Always on call. Just slipped to a side-room with a bunk for a nap. The interpreters in charge of each dormitory I met every morning at 6am. Before that I already had their written reports, collected and analysed by one very special girl. She really was exceptional. Probably slept even less than I did.

These interpreters were briefed on the day's program, co-ordinated with the other sections.

However, it was not all so innocent. One day, during the festival an elderly major came to my office for a private talk. We slipped down to the nearest café. He told me to ask the interpreters I was working with to look around for somebody amongst the foreign visitors they thought might be suitable to work for Czech Intelligence. I didn't know what to reply. I did not know this officer. I wanted to check who he is. I contacted the person I could most trust, Lada Novak. He introduced me to Osvald Zavodsky, who was Chief of Intelligence in the communist party. Lada served with Zavodsky in the Czech brigade during the Spanish civil war. To get to

Zavodsky, passed a few doors and finally entered a huge vault. After all the building was a bank. Had I not been with Lada I would have been scared. Osvald left the room and when he returned, said: It's OK, you can trust him. Meeting the major again, he received me with a smile. I understood he knew I had checked on him. The instructions were; only to speak to interpreters I trust and only singly. They in turn should also be careful, who they approach, also singly. Make a sort of fleeting remark, as though in jest. Any-one hooked would be handed a telephone number to make contact.

The social side of the festival was great. Just to imagine thousands of young people from all over the world coming together two years after the end of the most horrible war. There was a wonderful atmosphere of freedom and redemption. The delegation leaders arrived a couple of weeks before the festival started and our entertainment started right then. The students in charge of entertainment arranged outings to beauty spots, general sightseeing, tickets to concerts and other cultural events. First a get-together of all the delegation Heads, 32 of them. This they organized outdoors at a beautiful spot on the river, near Mšeno. How well I remembered this place from the outings when we were kids, to see the cherries blossom in May. We were extremely lucky with the weather, not a drop of rain the whole time. During the three weeks of the festival, the two big European delegations, French and Italian, changed every week.

Each group stayed just a week and another one came the same day. Their leaders stayed throughout the time of the festival.

I tried to mix with as many delegation members as possible. There were two delegations from Palestine, one was a Zionist group, the other a left-wing group comprising Mapam members and Arabs. One of the Zionist group I met years later a number of times at a mutual friend. Six youngsters from England, who had hitch-hiked across Europe, arrived a couple of weeks before the official start of the festival. Though nothing was ready yet, they were well looked after, with housing, interpreters and entertainment. John, one of these boys, I met a few months later at LSE, where we both studied.

The Head of the British delegation was Les Canon. He came from Wigan, was an executive member of the Electrical Trade Union. We became very good friends and months later he often attended meetings at the Czechoslovak-British Friendship League in London. He was a staunch communist. Disillusioned he resigned from the party in 1956 when the Russians marched into Budapest. I was surprised he didn't do so after the Slánský trial.

The Canadian delegation were all from Toronto. I met them again in autumn of the same year, when I came to their town. From Norway, just one girl. With the leaders of the most numerous Italian delegation, De La Setta and

Luciana Francinetti, I met   frequently. Luciana was as beautiful as her name.

An interpreter with the American delegation asked me if it is possible that the Americans eat dogs. They were asking him where they can get *hot dogs*.

One of the main events of the festival was a big parade with all the delegations marching through the main streets of Prague to a central arena, where there would be speeches by the organizers and other dignitaries. On the morning of the parade, one of the interpreters called me with a problem. They had found an American girl in possession of Zionist leaflets, which she meant to distribute during the parade. The last thing we wanted, was political conflicts.

I told the interpreter to keep her confined to her room. It didn't take long, that I received a telephone call from Steinhardt, the American Ambassador, who accused us of holding an American citizen against her will. I assured him that I was not holding anybody, but would look into the matter.

I rang up my colleagues and instructed them to let the girl go, but confiscate all the leaflets, and make sure she didn't have any more on her. I called Steinhardt and told him what had transpired. I also told him I would be interested in meeting with him. He could not agree. In those days the Americans were so anti-communist that the Ambassador was afraid to meet with me. In fact, we both could have got into trouble. However, I told him about the Zionist leaflets and explained that we could not allow them to be distributed for political reasons, not because of anti-Semitism. To strengthen my explanation, I added that I was both Jewish and a Zionist. During that short talk I told him about the mistaken attitude of the State Department towards the Czech communist party. We have no intention to be Stalin's lackeys. He must have known how wrong I was. Czechoslovakia was already sold at Yalta to belong to the Soviet orbit. Laurance Steinhardt as US ambassador helped John Pehle of the War Refugee Board and Ira Hirschmann of Bloomingdale's to rescue more than 100,000 Jews from Hungary, Romania and Bulgaria.

At the end of the festival, I went to the Minister of Information, Václav Kopecky. I had been given a budget to cover the cost of the interpreters and I had not spent it all. I asked the Minister if I could divide the money amongst those who had worked so hard during the festival. He agreed and we parted on good terms, but not before he handed me my passport as he had promised in addition a remuneration, which I changed into 1,000 English pounds, then $ 5,000. I was now free to go.

I returned to Czechoslovakia with great hope to participate building an even better country than it was before the war. A much better social structure and fairer economic system. And it seemed going that way, right from the beginning. The atmosphere of democratic freedom gave me a feeling of pleasure and happiness. This was, that bound me, increased my feeling of belonging to the Czech country. What a difference from England, Canada and the USA, where my being Jewish was a handicap. Now I left, but didn't leave for good, just for studies in England. Studies with the comfort of being with my parents. To have a home. Vodička's offer to increase my rank to Major, sounded attractive, but it didn't mean to actually having a higher position than I had as a lieutenant. What it did mean, two stars surrounded by a golden braid on my shoulders. To study at the Frunze military academy was even more attractive, had it been near Prague. I disliked the Stalinist system, to have to weigh every word I utter. I wanted, my studies to get me a position at the Ministry of Foreign Affairs or Ministry of Foreign Trade. Had things not changed so drastically, that was for me a realistic possibility.

## Chapter 10: Svoboda !

Once I had rejected Brno and Moscow, off to London, where the rest of my family lived, and commence my studies at the London School of Economics.

I had received all necessary permits from the authorities, allowing me to study in England. To get such a permit I had to get recommendations. I got one from my old acquaintance Nosek (Minister of Interior). He also arranged for me to meet Nejedly, Minister of Education. I was free to go, but asked to keep in touch with the Czechoslovak Embassy in London. The person I was meeting weekly was the embassy's first secretary Edvard Goldstücker. We discussed current affairs and he kept me up-to-date about developments in Prague. My first visit in London was to the Midland Bank in Regent street, where I had my wartime savings, meaning the salaries I received from the RAF. My object to add the thousand pounds to my account. The account had been closed and all the money withdrawn; by my sister. I couldn't believe it. I gave Steffi the right to sign as a precaution in case I get killed, for the family to get hold of my money easily. I opened another account. Cannot walk with a thousand pounds in my pocket!

There was a British-Czechoslovak Friendship League in London, controlled by the Prague government I was asked to become involved. The head of that League was a Sudeten German, Mr Hampel. Apart from its propaganda function, the organization also represented some of the Czech industries. Soon I became Hampel's assistant. I travelled to various places in England on behalf of the League, advertising Czechoslovakia. One of the members was a Czech actor, Herbert Lom. I met him regularly, yet he did not wish his association to be known. Did not attend any meetings. We only met privately. We had quite a number of members and supporters, some well-known personalities. MP Sinclair was very active and I believe that after Hampel and I left, he ran the Friendship League. Then there was Colonel Wigg, who was Parliamentary Secretary to the Home Secretary Emmanuel Shinwell. I got Les Canon to join.

Our tutor for International Relations was from the British Foreign Office. He knew exactly what my political leanings were. After February 1948, when Czechoslovakia embarked on a one party system, to which I too took exception, the same tutor tried to persuade me to make a political statement against the new Czech government. In return he would see to it that I get a British passport. I could have had such a passport after the war, having served in the RAF.

Though during the war I was impressed by what Britain did and I did my duty, participating in the fight against Britain's and our enemy, my views took a drastic change due to the war Britain waged against Jews trying to reach Palestine. There was a social change as well; anti-

Semitism lifted its head again. My parents' house was in 23 Norrice Lea (Hampstead Garden Suburbs). When on leave, I played tennis at a club which was nearly opposite my parents' house. They were always only too pleased to arrange a game for me when I showed up during the war in my RAF uniform. Back in England in 1947, they were happy I applied for membership at the very same tennis club. Entering my address on the application form they knew the house belonged to a Jewish family. When asked how come I live there, I told them this is my parents' house. Realizing I am Jewish, the whole atmosphere changed. Suddenly there was *a waiting list, there were many applicants that came before you.* After Prague, where such an attitude was unacceptable, I saw Britain in a different light. Thus I was not over-enthusiastic about taking British citizenship. I also believed the one party rule would not last long in Czechoslovakia and I would be back, soon.

Although my father had set up a business in England in 1939, which was doing well, both he and my mother were not sure if they wanted to stay in the British Isles. There was no point in going back to Teplice. The old Teplice was gone and none of their old friends had returned. There were problems with the post-war agreements between the Russians and the Allies. To reach West Berlin, one had to cross the Russian zone and the Russians would not allow anyone through. Everything had to be done by air. Renewed confrontation was a distinct possibility. Father started playing with the idea of going to Canada.

I was the one to scout the land. At this same visit I tried to find out my chances to study at McGill University, as all the family was now planning to move to Canada. I had anticipated this move before leaving Prague, where I had already completed one year's study at Charles University. The Prague Dean gave me a letter of recommendation for the Dean of McGill's, a friend of his. That was great. Never expected to be received in such a forthcoming way. The Dean asked me about his friend in Prague, general developments and about my past. My service in the RAF impressed him. I was sure there would be no problem for me to be accepted at his university. Everything was going smoothly. The Dean then said *my Prague friend says in his letter, you would like to study at our University .Yes*, I said. *What do I have to do, in order to be accepted ? You don't have to do anything, I'll do all the formalities for you*. He called his secretary to bring an application form, and the Dean himself filled out the form. Asked the questions on the application form and I replied. Came the question *race*. I remembered what Jan Masaryk, Foreign Minister of Czechoslovakia, wrote when confronted with the same question, going to the USA. **Human** he wrote. This is the answer I gave. However, I was no Jan Masaryk, just Peter Arton, and suddenly, like at the tennis club, there the famous **waiting list**.

My sister's husband was an excellent engineer. During the war he worked in the aircraft industry in England. He was also the co-inventor of the container for the flame-thrower. After the war, father gave him and his partner an office in the building father had leased on 31, Finsbury Square. My brother-in-law and his partner were tool makers. They designed the first tools to manufacture ball-point pens. That it did not succeed, like many first invention, had to do with the conservatism with the main consumers. In this case it was the banks. They would not accept a signature with this new gadget. With all his excellent recommendations, my brother-in-law had problems in Canada.

I tried to find out his chances of employment in Montreal, applied to an agency which specialized in placing engineers. They asked me if he was Jewish. *Many companies don't want to employ Jews.* This just a short time after the horrors of WWII had been revealed. Nothing affected deep-rooted anti-Semitism. In the end, when Harry came over, he was accepted at Canadair, Canada's leading aircraft factory. He rose there eventually to the highest position, Executive Vice President.

Everything changed in February 1948, as the Communists took over in Prague. A group of us met at the Czechoslovak Embassy, discussing the recent events. Opinions differed. But even Goldstücker, a communist since his student days, did   not like this development. The changes were drastic. Mr Zeman, representing the Ministry of the Interior at the Embassy, was called to Prague for consultations. After a couple of weeks there was still no sign of him. I asked why he had not come back. Nobody knew.

After another couple of weeks someone else came and took his place. All our questions about Zeman's whereabouts were evaded. Gradually I realized, Zeman had disappeared, the usual Russian way. There is a lot of space in Siberia.

In 1948, Hampel organized a visit to Prague for an English trade union delegation. On his return he was given two weeks by the British authorities to tie up his affairs, and was expelled from Britain. I was called to the embassy. Goldstücker and the Ambassador greeted me and without too much formality asked me to take over the Czech Friendship League. I felt I could not refuse their request.

I told my tutor at LSE about my new position. A few days later he called me to his office. *If you do, you'll be thrown out of Britain.* I reported this warning to the Ambassador and Dr Goldstücker. They arranged a meeting at the embassy together with M.P. Sinclair and Colonel Wigg. I intended to go to Canada and did not want to be refused re-entry to the UK. I knew about the not so friendly relation between the Home Secretary

Shinwell and the Foreign Secretary Bevin. The last thing I wanted to be in the middle of a fight between them. Colonel Wigg's angry reaction to the warning I was given: *this is a matter for the Home Office, Bevin has no right to interfere.* Colonel Wigg told me, I shouldn't take any notice of the information from the Foreign Office. I asked him not to use me to get at Bevin and the Foreign Office. He gave me his word: *Don't worry, old chap, we won't mention it.*

With such a threat, there was no point taking the position at the Friendship League. The Embassy people agreed with me. They didn't want the embarrassment of another Czech citizen thrown out of the country.

I went to Canada, checked in at the Mount Royal Hotel. I hadn't been there five minutes when my phone started ringing and ringing. All the Montreal papers wanted to interview me. It didn't take me long to find out why. Despite all the promises, a statement had been made in the British parliament about the Foreign Office interfering in the work of the Home Office and my name was mentioned. I was furious. I called Colonel Wigg from Montreal and told him so. And *can I come back to Britain?* I asked. He would not give me an answer immediately, but promised to let me know. A few days later I received Colonel Wigg's call: *There will be no problem for you to come back to England.*

I had come to Montreal to possibly find apartments for parents and Steffi + family. I found two apartments in a new building in Cote St Luc. Parents came over. From London, father had already negotiated with a fur manufacturer about entering his business. Now he perfected the deal and became Mr. Shlomovic's partner. Father asked Steffi to sell the house in Norrice Lea. He needed the money, to invest in the new business. It was unfortunate that I was not in London at the time. After all, I also lived in that house and Steffi didn't have the sense to ask me if I had something there, a part of my clothing. Thus I lost a very important document. My diary I had kept from the day we left Teplice till I reached England.

## Chapter 11: Prague Visit

After my visit to Canada, I felt at odds what to do. With parents' house sold, I didn't have where to stay. The salary I could have got for running the Czech League, was out. Nor did I particularly want to stay in England. Henry was in London running father's business. He and his wife Cynthia lived in a very smart small apartment at Knightsbridge, corner Sloane street. Canada was out, as I could not study there. I decided to go to Prague on a look-and-see visit. I had not been since the communist takeover. Recalling the Zeman episode, I wanted to cover myself before leaving. I asked Zeman's replacement to try and procure an exit permit for me, before I depart from London. It was a new rule that no Czech citizen can leave his country without such an exit permit.

The exit visa in hand, I set off for Prague in December 1948. The first day there, I contacted a very good friend from university and many party meetings, Jiři Pelikan. (This is the same person, who was head of Czech television during the Prague Spring 1967. He kept on broadcasting against the Russian invasion. For the Russians not to get hold of him he was posted to the Czech Embassy in Rome). After the war he was very active in the students' union together with a childhood friend of mine from Teplice, Edgar Semmel. During the war, Edgar was in the Czechoslovak army in England and we met frequently.

Jiři was very happy to see me. He had set up a press conference for the next day with some American and British reporters and members of foreign embassies. Jiři was the main speaker and as he spoke only Czech, he asked me to interpret for him into English. I protested. I knew I was very bad in interpreting. With the press conference due to take place the next day he did not succeed to find anyone to help him out. I obliged. I'm sure I made a very bad job of it. Worse, as I saw the unfriendly, even inimical expressions on the foreign audience.

That evening we went out together to a nightclub, named *7P*. Every table had a number in big letters and a telephone next to it. The idea was to dial the number of a table with the girl one fancied. If lucky, she wasn't rude.

We left the club in the early hours of the morning. I was shocked by the scene I witnessed. The first sign of the ugly side of the new Czechoslovakia. Men with red armbands trying to break into shops, shouting for the owners to open up. I didn't understand what they intended to achieve. Nobody is there at night. They banged away at the shutters, and then went to the next shop for a repeat performance. Jiři was embarrassed. Just a few hours ago he had said at the press conference that *Czechoslovakia continues its democratic tradition.* When I asked Jiři why the police doesn't interfere, he had nothing to say. I was now less sure why I came here. I shuddered at the thought that the victim of such vandalism could have been my father had he returned to Czechoslovakia. Memories of Kristallnacht came flooding back to me. Still, I carried on as intended. Visited some of my old haunts and some of my friends from the time I was in Prague. Could I re-adjust? Bedřich Hájek from the cadre department was quite blunt. *You would be regarded too much of a security risk – You had been in the West for too long, and the fact that your parents are there doesn't help matters.*

Where could I fit in? I went from ministry to ministry. I saw Evžen Loebl, deputy Minister of Foreign Trade. Kopecky, Minister of Information, Nejedly, minister of Education. They all gave me some options and I parted saying I'll think it over.

I contacted Josef Baudyš. He was still at communist party headquarters. We had a very long talk. We had been very close and he told me a number of confidential things. At a security meeting, the Czech security guys listened to a lecture by a Russian expert. This is the idea he brought across, *somebody suspected of anti-state activities, should be left alone, to give him a chance to recruit others and then bounce on the whole group.* Baudyš protested *these are Gestapo methods which we don't plan to introduce.* Baudyš then told me the Russians are trying very hard we should copy them. After some time they'll give up and let us run our affairs. It won't take long.

If I had my choice, my preference would be to work with the Ministry of Foreign Trade, or Ministry of Foreign Affairs, providing I could stay abroad. At this stage I was set to get a job abroad only, not in Czechoslovakia. I would return after the Russian influence evaporated, blow over, and things return to normal. I went to see Evžen Loebl again. When I returned to the Formans, where I stayed (there I also lived before leaving for England) I was told Osvald Zavodsky rang me to come to see him. *I think Intelligence should be your choice. You're familiar with the West, speak English and German.*

Zavodsky set up interviews for me with high officials of the Foreign Office. They asked many questions, wanting to get acquainted with me. I did not know them before. Alone with Osvald again, he told me to cut my involvement with the Friendship League, cut my ties with Goldstücker and the Czechoslovak Embassy altogether. Concentrate on my university studies, keep a low profile, and you'll be contacted after we decided on a position for you. One more thing they told me: Apply for a British passport. Zavodsky asked me to leave my communist party card with him *nobody will ever know that you are a party member.*

I didn't react, didn't carry it any further, didn't ask questions. What did go through my head; on the one hand, because of my life in the West, my family in the

West, I couldn't be trusted,    suddenly I could be asked to take on an assignment that presupposes supreme trust. True, Lada my closest war time friend could have influenced Osvald. And Osvald was after all the top security man.

My next thought was to keep my appointment with a girlfriend at a coffee house, just a few steps from Osvald's office. We discussed the day before to spend a few days skiing at Spindlerův Mlýn, a ski resort in the highest Bohemian mountains, Krkonoše. Now we finalized our plan.

Many years later, with Sally, made a stop-over at Ingolstadt in Germany. In the hotel lobby was a big poster with a hotel I had seen before. It was the best known hotel in Spindler Mühle. I started to sing **Riesengebierge, deutsches Gebierge** the receptionist joined in, **meine schöne Heimat Du.** The owners of that hotel were her parents. She was just a child, when she and her family were expelled.

Returning to the Formans pretty late in the evening, Mrs Forman told me, that Bedřich Hajek wanted to see me urgently and a message from the Prague secretary of the communist party, messages from people who didn't leave their name. All wanted to see me. With all the many urgent messages, not knowing what it is all about, I panicked. Don't really know why. In the back of my mind always the people disappearing for no reason. I was

afraid to even find out  what it is all about. That
night I checked in at hotel Juliš under a false name. All I
wanted was to get out quickly before any-one finds out
that I have an exit permit! The next morning I took the
Orient Express to Paris. I was very tense, afraid I could
be stopped at the border. As the train crossed the Czech
border I relaxed. I now thought, I may have over-reacted.
Perhaps there was nothing to it, maybe just another talk
or a decision of a position for me. Too late to do anything
about it. From Paris I took a plane to London.

I really wasn't thinking straight, but once I got back to
London, I did what Osvald told me. I called on Edward
Goldstücker and told him I intended to cut my ties with
the Friendship League, because of all the problems it
caused me. The same goes for my close relation with the
Embassy. I answered all his subsequent questions very
vaguely, something so unlike me. I am sure he knew I am
not telling him the truth.

Only Henry and his wife, were in London. Cynthia, the
daughter of a typically *British* retired colonel, retired
from his Indian service. I had to look for digs. Mr Kraus,
a Czech professor, I was friendly with, found me a
suitable place. A room where I had to insert a coin to get
it heated for warmth and hot water.

During the war, father had a good textile business
(whole-sale of worsted fabrics) in London. The offices
were on the ground floor as was the warehouse of

worsteds. The basement was used for storing rayon linings. On the first floor small textile items were manufactured, mainly for the army. A very able manager, also Czech, ran the production as an independent unit. During the war one could make money on anything. The business that father bought went under the name of H&B Clothiers. He then bought an existing converting business "Max & Bourne". This company , dealing with linings for outer garments, had a quota of supplies from Scovill, a factory in Nelson, near Manchester. To get goods, even after the war, was the number one problem. Each week the same quantity of linings, in-the-grey, was delivered to a finishing plant in Paisley, Scotland. They would finish the fabric and dye it to father's instructions and send it to the London warehouse. It also went well during the first couple of years after the war. Then the game changed, as more and more goods were produced. No longer supplies was the problem, but marketing. Father looked for new ways, new outlets. Summer 1947, together with a neighbour in Hampstead Garden Suburbs, he devised an idea to open a shop on Broadway, New-York and sell worsted fabrics in suit lengths, mainly for tailors as well as individual buyers. Father was the one to put up the money, US$ 50,000, then a very considerable sum. It didn't worry father that this particular neighbour, did not have a very good reputation. To my question, if that doesn't worry him, he answered he won't do anything wrong, he needs me. Father came back without a business and without the money.

As long as parents were in London I lived in their house. My expenses were minimal. This now changed. I could not count on it to ever get my war-time savings back from my dear sister so my only reserve was the money I brought from Czecho savings. I had most of my meals at Henry, though Cynthia was not exactly a gourmet cook. Henry's plan was to go to Canada as well and asked me to familiarize myself with the business and keep an eye on it during his absence.

By now it was the beginning of 1949. I was continuing my studies and come to Henry to learn about the business. I could see it wasn't doing well. We went through the books. The business owed money to a number of suppliers. After a long discussion we decided on the obvious; ring all our creditors and tell them we have to delay payment. Fortunately they were very understanding, having worked with Father for many years. This we couldn't do with Scovill, the Max&Bourne supplier in Nelson. Every Friday we received his invoice, which he sent the same morning, we sent the cheque and on that same Friday afternoon Scovill got it. In those days the postal service was excellent. Five mail deliveries a day in the City.

Not to pay, would mean closing down the converting outfit, the only really stable business we had.

Henry had borrowed 5,000 pounds from his father-in-law, which he sunk into the business. He couldn't just leave without some arrangement to repay this. So I guaranteed re-payment on a monthly basis, without a clue how I could.

I decided to apply for British citizenship. After filling out all the forms I had to find two sponsors. The colonel, Henry's father-in-law, was one, and the professor who helped me find accommodation, was the other. Although Czech, he had already obtained his British citizenship many years ago.

To try to save the business, I had to become more involved and neglected my studies because of it. Eventually I abandoned them altogether. With Henry we had to find a way to economize. The first-floor manufacturing unit we decided to close down as it just held itself over the water, bringing no profit. It was very good before, making collars for men's shirts. Instead of changing the whole shirt, only the collar had to be changed and affixed to the shirt with studs, like our Air Force shirts. It was run as an independent unit by a very efficient manager. Not his fault that demand had dropped so drastically. Maybe he should have tried to find alternative articles with more demand. Henry and I were too inexperienced to think of new ideas and not ready to experiment.

Henry was friendly with the Mohans, two Indian brothers, cotton importers. They rented the whole first floor, now empty. This more than covered the expenses of the Finsbury house.

March 1949 Henry and Cynthia left for Canada. I took over Henry's apartment in Sloane Street. I continued to economize to such an extend, as to walk a lot instead of taking a bus or tube. Economizing on the staff was my next step. There were two secretaries. The pretty one in the early thirties, I let go first. She was very busy with private calls and I didn't think I needed two girls anyway. Then there was an elderly accountant and a man in charge of the warehouse. One of the secretary's most time consuming function, writing letters. Come summer, my secretary took her holiday break. Manpower sent a temporary replacement. Jeanette, a 17 year old girl. Excellent, is not the word. Out of this world. As her two weeks were about to come to an end, I asked her if she wouldn't like to stay as my permanent secretary. Getting her positive answer, I asked Manpower. They agreed to let her go.

With no Telex, Fax, Computer, E-mail, the typewriter was *king*. First thing in the morning I dictated letters, got them back for signature a day or two later. This was the case with the two previous secretaries. Jeanette finished the correspondence within a couple of hours. I went to her office as I just couldn't understand how she does it.

She was typing at machine   gun speed and no mistakes to erase. The girls took down in shorthand, what I dictated. Whilst the previous girls always asked me to slow down, for Jeanette I was dictating too slowly.

The next problem, I didn't know that it can be solved. Whenever I wanted to know a client's or supplier's balance, it took the accountant twenty, thirty minutes to give me an answer. This is the way the business was run since 1939. Out of the blue, my auditor rang to tell me his younger brother wants to meet me, as he is taking over my account. He was much younger, probably not much older than myself. He had finished his studies recently, interrupted by the war. He had served in the 8th Army, came all the way from Egypt along North Africa, Sicily to Italy. After war stories, we came to my problem. Jerry explained, my elderly accountant, uses the Continental system of one ledger, sales, purchases, expenses in one book. The English system is much more practical. Have each of these activities in separate books. Jeanette said she can do it. A number of meetings with Jerry, and Jeanette took over the book keeping. As the business grew we added her sister to the staff and no more delays.

After I left England, Jeanette stayed on, till the business closed down, after father passed away in 1957

Having managed to reduce expenses was important but to increase sales, much more so. The linings kept me going. But that was not enough. Many salesmen came every day. I expertly bought the    wrong goods at the wrong price. When an old buddy from my squadron came to offer some worsted fabrics; I bought. After all, him I can trust! He represented a mill in Bradford. I bought quite a quantity. Got stuck with the whole lot.

Two months after Henry left I hit the jackpot.

One of Father's business contacts was Sydney Lewis. He had cotton mills in Manchester, owned Mercury Bicycles in Birmingham. Sidney was a very hardworking man. He lived in a South London suburb. Daily by train to Charring Cross Road. Had his shoes cleaned by the same shoe-shine boy and was at his Regent street office much before his staff. An avid football fan, Saturdays found him at Highbury, the Arsenal football ground. He had his permanent seat.

I saw Sidney pretty often, before going to Finsbury street. I bought from him and he was my biggest buyer of linings. Despite the age difference, we liked each other's company. Maybe he hoped I could be his future son-in-law. Didn't like his daughter's choice of a much older man. But that was the man his daughter did marry.

Sydney called me one day. Another gentleman I knew, was also present. Sir Cecil Douglas, a director of his company. Sydney came up with a proposition. Nylon stockings were in great demand. However, supply fell well short of demand. I couldn't even try to dream of such a business. I didn't have the necessary contacts or the big money this required. Sidney had the contacts, he bought large quantities of ladies' cotton stockings The same mills produced nylon stockings but these they would only supply as a percentage of the quantity one could buy for export. This was a Government regulation, as Britain was trying desperately to build up her foreign currency reserves. This then was the idea. I should find foreign buyers and would get a share of the local sales. Export could be done nearly at cost. The profit would bring the local market. Sir Cecil Douglas, a man with great influence and good connections would worry about supplies, I about export sales.

To me this was the irony of ironies – Father had been busy making ladies' stockings way back in the 1920s in Teplice and here was his son in the same business in London 30 years later.

Not much effort for me to discover that Belgium was the country to concentrate on. Belgium did issue import licenses for such goods. So to Brussels I flew. Checked in at the elegant Metropol hotel, in the town centre. Went to see hosiery shops and department stores, to get an idea of prices, visited a number of wholesalers. I could certainly sell large quantities of nylons. There was a snag. Import licences. Snag number two. With the import license application, 10% of the license value had to be deposited with the authorities and only a Belgian resident could obtain such a license. English mills already selling in Belgium did so to clients with Import Licenses. I had another idea. Find some-one reliable enough to trust, give him the money required to get a License and let him do the marketing. A week I spent in Brussels. At one of the prospective buyers I found the man I was looking for. Mr. Vicze , a Hungarian immigrant. I invited him for dinner with his very beautiful wife. Vicze's big, well going business in Budapest, he lost. Hungary was now run on communist lines. I couldn't have found a better man.

We went ahead. I gave Mr. Vicze money to apply for an Import License, in his name. By Airfreight Sydney now shipped weekly lots of nylon stockings. I found myself traveling backwards and forwards to Belgium. I was in Bruxelles as soon as goods were cleared. Mr. Vicze distributed them, collected the money and took new orders. Our clients now had one great advantage, didn't need to apply for import licenses. That got me a large clientele, all I needed were goods. The export business brought very little profit. The profit was on the home market, which Sydney looked after. The demand was tremendous. I was making money. Bought my first car, an Austin 16, over 10 years old. There were no new cars. All were exported. .

I returned Henry's debt to  his father-in law in one lump sum. The Colonel looked at my largesse with suspicion.

## Chapter 12: Spy school

Soon after Henry and Cynthia left I had a call. The person on the line said how he enjoyed the pastries at a certain café. All this in Czech. He went on in a joyous way and mentioned regards from Osvald Zavodsky.

We arranged to meet. My contact gave me a code name Valsorim, He also gave me an emergency address in Prague to remember Karel Valicek, POBox160, Prague 7. My contact assumed I was in. He didn't ask me if I was prepared to work for them. I felt too nervous to protest or ask questions. I felt the safest thing would be just to go along. The purpose of this preliminary talk, how to communicate and meet in the future. The way I should understand the day, the time. How to leave messages in a phone booth or under a bench. Dead drops. Just dry runs. Innocent, innocuous texts. For this I needed a good camera. He suggested I buy a Leica. He gave me 1,500 pounds. He made me sign for it. He explained how to photograph messages and written documents and how to develop the film. That was easy, everything was black and white. Didn't need the sophisticated machinery of today. I had developed films on my own before, so had some experience. Once the film was developed, to apply a chemical and scrub until the hard part of the film was removed and a very soft and flimsy substance remained. This would leave the photographed part undamaged.

The next stage was to leave it for the pick-up. At a pre-arranged time and place, would fix the film with chewing gum underneath the rack holding the telephone directories in a phone box. Always at a different phone box, but never far from home or business. I bought the camera and we commenced in the practice runs. I photographed pages of any book I happened to have. The drop and the pick-up had to be precise. Avoid the risk of a member of the public going into the booth and casually running his hands under the directory rack, and find our little package!

Dead drops was the only way to communicate. Telephoning was out. Anyway I didn't have any number to call. Then I was taught a very simple code. Simple but hard to detect. We decided on a certain paragraph of a certain page of a pre-arranged book. Very simple and very secure. Apart from that we kept on changing pages. I got some simple exercises to practice how to apply the code. Spy-school by correspondence !

Business kept on going extremely well. I discovered something new. It bothered me. It bothered me because it was contrary to my outlook, my conception, my believe, my trust that socialism is the answer to everything that is evil. I danced with the people when the Socialists won the first post-war election in England. After the war the U.K. was by far the greatest industrial power in Europe. Industry not only intact, even enlarged. It had such an enormous industrial *Vorsprung.* The big competitors, Germany, Italy, France had to start from scratch. England should have been able to take-off at top speed. It didn't happen. Restrictions and more restrictions. Rules for the sake of rules. Armies of bureaucrats have to check and control. Every three months an inspector came to check with me how much Purchase Tax I have to pay. How many such well-trained accountants had to be used ! These armies have to be paid. High income tax is the answer. That is not all. The people must be protected. Keep the cost down. Regulate profit. Our lining converting company *Max&Borne* was allowed to make a 5% profit. The whole-sale business *H&B Clothiers* 12.5%. There was a strict price control. But what business can run on such limited profits! I discovered the sad news. A country's economy cannot be run on socialist principles.

Every few weeks I travelled to Nelson, near Manchester to pay my supplier 200% above his permitted price in cash. I had to do likewise with my clients. That was the result. A black economy. Normal business was throttled. Income-tax was ridiculously high. There was a loop-hole. To buy a company that has accumulated losses. Throw all the profits into that company, tax free. The going price of such a company was 10% of the book loss. I bought a hosiery company that showed a considerable loss. I kept the son of the owner to run the outfit, left the business in the same, very good location, in Regent street, very near

Sidney's office. John was very good, knew the business and happy to be able to continue. Dealt with all types of hosiery items, from lisle stockings to underwear. I helped to increase sales by exporting to my nylon clients in Europe.

From a reliable source I was told, Belgium will stop issuing Import Licenses for nylon stockings. My reaction, I asked Vicze to apply for a considerably larger quantity of nylons to import. I often met the salesmen of the competing English nylon manufacturers and as import licenses were no longer issued, they approached me with a problem. Their system of selling to clients with an import license was money-wise better. But now they were in trouble. They had goods in Brussels but no clients with import licenses. I was on top of the world. They asked me to help them with Vicze's licenses. I wasn't very much interested. Then Sidney called me that people from the Board of Trade asked to help these manufacturers. I came to the meeting. Now it was a different story. If we help we were promised a much bigger allocation of nylons for the local market. Also accepted our condition, not to sell to my clients in Belgium. In fact, these manufacturers could just throw away their nylon stock in Belgium and would still be left with a handsome profit. They just couldn't disclose to the authorities that the big part of the profit they don't declare.

I didn't neglect my social life. Befriended sons of business people, of manufacturers, some who I was working with. I went swimming, played tennis, squash. Went to balls in a smoking-jacket, mainly charity balls in support of the new Israel. At professor Kraus I met a very intelligent young man, just a few years older than myself. The son of the very well-to-do, pre-war Czech liqueur company. Wantoch joined me. He was a great asset. I was no longer alone. Had some-one to talk to, discuss with. He was all the time at my side. Through him I got to know a Czech actress, Nora Svojsíková. She had come with a group of Czech actors to a film festival in London. She decided to defect and stay in England. Very pretty. I fell for her. Here I am with a film star and I prefer to go to the theatre, opera, concerts, not movies. We went for week-ends to the south coast, Bornmouth, Torquay, Eastbourne. We went to see Stonehenge with the brothers Hakim, I was friendly with from LSE. They were the sons of Egypt's Minister of Foreign Affairs.

Czech Intelligence must have forgotten about me. Mention the devil. I got a call from which I understood where to collect a message. I was given an address in Bradford to give a Miss Schoenova 30 pounds for a radio. The next time I had to go to Nelson, I checked in at the Midland hotel in Manchester, as I always did. Wantoch was with me. I always came in the evening and drove to Nelson the following morning. I went to my room, Wantoch to his. Then I slipped out for the most horrible journey. Never crossed the Pennines before. Maybe nice during a sunny day. But this was a stormy, rainy night. In Bradford, as planned by a map, I left the car quite a distance away from the intended address. It was after 11 pm when I knocked at Miss Schoenova's door. She took a long time to answer. When she did, I realised this wasn't the right moment to pay a visit. She was hurriedly wrapping a robe around her. Behind her stood a half-naked young man. I asked her an innocent question, as advised in the note. Her answer was correct. I gave her the money and left.

Coincidentally, my father engaged this young man as a salesman a couple of years later. I am quite sure it was a coincidence. He did not recognize me. Neither did I. The penny dropped after being told he had lived in Bradford. I couldn't tell father and so he stayed and was very successful. After I was arrested he came to my father to tell him how sorry he is. He knew about Schoenova being questioned by police. Had he known it concerns me, he would have told her to shut up. Only many years later I realised it wouldn't have made any difference. It was a pre-arranged set-up, coordinated by the Soviet-Czech-British Intelligence.

As a matter of fact, my visit to Bradford was actually my one and only intelligence task I performed. Everything else was being taught *how to*. It was ludicrous really. Usually Intelligence people and spies attend special schools and courses and   are taught all aspects of the profession. Never had any training! I met with my contact three or four times.

At the end of 1949, I was invited to go to Stockholm to meet the boss. I went. Checked in at the Grand Hotel, a very fine hotel in the center of Stockholm. It was early in the afternoon that I wanted to have a look what Stockholm looks like. There is a wide stairway to descend to the pavement. As I got out, a large crowd of people started clapping. Not for me. Behind me was Gregory Peck.

I rented a car, but returned it again soon after. Sweden had changed to driving on the right side, to which I was not used. Then, for the first time I saw those loop entries and exits plus the wrong side, I couldn't manage. Lucky to get back to the hotel, returned the car. For business visits, a taxi would be much more reliable. Very odd, I met very few people speaking English or German. Maybe the hotel concierge was right that German is much more common but people want to forget their close war-time relation with Nazi Germany. Thus reluctant to speak that language.

With the boss I walked for miles. Took sightsee boat trips to the numerous islands. It rained all the time. I had to buy new shoes every couple of days because my shoes were getting saturated.

The punch line, I was not needed in England. I should carry on with my business and prepare to move to the Argentine. I was even given the name of a secretary at the Argentine Embassy to approach. No rush. Take your time. Now the basic, the most important part for which I was called to Sweden. *You never went through intelligence training and that is not what we need you for. We followed your business success and business is what I want to discuss with you.*

We did not go into details, but I understood my business in Buenos Aires will correspond with Czech concerns, as well, with the view to become their sole agent. Not just textiles, also crystal, machinery and other exportable items. As well as advancing the export of Argentinean goods to Czechoslovakia. Businesswise an excellent proposition. They would help me with marketing by sending *technicians* of the various suppliers

Whilst in Sweden I may as well try to find clients. Had free mornings. Why, I don't know. Saw quite a number of department stores and wholesalers. I offered mainly nylon stockings and fine English worsteds and tweeds for men's suits. Items, very much in demand and in short supply all over Europe. With England's reputation for quality, it shouldn't be difficult to sell. Yet I never experienced such a cold reception by all I approached. Extremely conservative. *We have our suppliers* and that was it. Just couldn't break the ice.

Generally speaking, I was at ease, pleasant to speak with my very intelligent boss. Discussed everything. I asked many questions of how the change of February 48 influenced the general situation. Mentioned my experience in Prague at the end of 48. No, he did not avoid to discuss the most awkward subjects. I did not ask him outright if he is against the undue Russian pressure. After all, the Czechoslovak government agreed to join the Marshall plan, had to abandon it. Eugen Löbl told us they had decided to buy Volvo trucks instead of Russian ones. He gave reasons: better payment terms and reliability in getting spare parts. Löbl told us, he didn't accept Russian terms to sell uranium to the Soviet Union at a fixed price, yet get Russian wheat at world market prices. All was vetoed by the Russians. The boss's answers; to look at the broader picture, the West's unreliability in matters of security which Munich has taught us. (Löbl was one of the first arrested before the Slánský trial)

From all the talk, one request. I should not get married before I get to Argentina. I understood this to mean, to lose contact with England, which didn't worry me.

My business kept on growing. Not the lining business of Max & Bourne. The stock of linings was accumulating. I had the very large cellar, tiled, painted, put up shelves. Made it into a well organized warehouse. I stored the ever growing quantity of linings and waited for better times. Henry phoned from Canada, he had a very good outlet for these goods. I kept on shipping big quantities he asked for. I did not ask for payment, helping Henry to establish himself in the new country. As the Bank of England checked that money comes in for every export, I made arrangement with a Swiss bank to pay for the invoices. With my money.

January 1950. I felt I was now on firm ground. Knew father is not doing well. He had thrown all his money into this fur business. The promises of huge profits did not materialize. I phoned father, if it wasn't better to come back to England and help me with the business he knows. A few days and he came. He soon realized he is wasting his time in Canada. At first he wanted to return to Montreal, try to get money out of his fur business, but accepted my view it would be a waste of time and would probably only get promises. I persuaded him to go back, pack up everything and return with mother. It took just a couple of weeks for parents to be back. Henry's apartment was too small to house us all. We found a large apartment in 55 Portland Place, very posh locality. The previous tenant was a very wealthy, elderly gentleman, owner of the *Dunn* men's hat chain of stores. He had moved to the south coast because of his health. He was looking for a small pied-a-terre in London. Drove only Bentleys. We did a swap. He took the small apartment in Sloane Street, we moved into his.

Father's coming had an unexpected pleasant advantage. Being a foreign resident he could buy a new car for US dollars. A luxury not available for the local population. I bought a Humber. I had a new car for the first time ! Never again bought used cars, since.

I had accumulated a large cash reserve. Discussed with father how to secure it. My idea, to invest in real estate in Germany. Father felt sorry Steffi lived in a small apartment in Montreal. Why not invest in a house Steffi and family could live in and let them pay rental as soon as Harry's income increases. I discussed it with Steffi. Her idea, to buy a duplex, let the upper floor thus have an immediate income, which she will put in Fatchi's Montreal account. The question of trust was a question mark as Steffi had taken all my war savings and never returned a penny. I therefore suggested to make that deal with Henry. *Henry is a business man, he is able to manage. I will look after it that nothing goes wrong.* So my father. Steffi found a duplex in MacDonald street, I sent 75,000 dollars. Nothing went wrong, for Steffi. Father passed away prematurely, Steffi grabbed everything.

A problem I had to solve was, Nora. She wanted to get married. I was not ready to take such a step. Her best alternative she saw, to go back to Prague where her father was completely on his own. Her problem, she was scared to take that step as she had defected whilst on an official visit. It was now the first   time that I was the one to contact Czech Intelligence. I was assured she will not be harmed in any way. They kept their word. I found out from Eva, when she paid us a visit in 1968.

The new apartment, in Portland Place was very spacious, ideal for my parents, and within it there was a separate self-contained small apartment, perfect for me. From the former tenant we purchased the complete, very elegant, real Chippendale dining room suite. The whole of the master bedroom. Beautiful bed covers of a heavy pure silk and matching drapes. Same material on a stool in front of the beds. The same with the chair for the style toilet table. There also was a back-entrance, for service people and deliveries. This back-door led into a small self-contained apartment, bedroom, bathroom, small living room. This was the maid's abode. Her door led to the kitchen. Between the kitchen and the corridor leading to the main part of the apartment was a small room, the butler's pantry. We had a living-in maid, but no butler. I had the room wood panelled with benches and table of the same wood, turning it into an elegant breakfast room. I had this done whilst parents spent a few weeks in winter on the Canary Islands to escape the bad English weather.

I told father I was interested to set up a similar business in South America, preferably Buenos Aires. I went to see the secretary of the Argentine Embassy, as advised in Stockholm. The conversation was very down to earth.

About my business, how much I wished to invest in the Argentine. One thing was wrong. I had the feeling this Argentine Embassy official knew all about me. It seemed I am the only one not to know what it is all about. Am I getting into something I am not able to cope with? I thought about the experts who were to come to help me. Would they be sent for business only? If not, and one were caught. With my past, would anyone believe I had nothing to do with it?

I let it go, didn't persuade that direction any further. I was too busy with a growing business.

The first half of 1950 was not so great business wise. We experienced the first post-war recession. Then came the Korean War. Soon prices of all textiles sky rocketed. The weavers had a good time. They accepted orders for the coming couple of years at exorbitant prices. Wholesalers who fell for it had later a tough time to survive, as prices normalized. One of these unfortunate merchants, Steve, who I knew, went into bankruptcy. When his goods were taken to be auctioned, he came with a proposition. I should bid for his stock of the very fine worsted fabrics. His object, I let him sell those goods with a handsome commission for himself. I agreed.

Every interested party had to submit a written offer. I listened to Steve's suggestions. All those participating in the bidding were then invited to attend as the envelopes were being opened. We all sat in a room at a huge heavy table, seating some forty people. I was bidding against the big guys, representing the leading department stores. Yet, of the total of something over 70,000 pound I was the highest bidder for 62,000 pounds worth of goods. The goods that I was not interested in, were all ladies fabrics. The auctioneer wanted to know, who represents H&B Clothiers. I stood up. Not being known, he asked how I plan to pay such a big sum. I knew this question would arise, was ready for it. Put my attaché case on the table with cash in it. O.K. said the auctioneer. I'll accept your cheque.

I jumped at an opportunity to buy another wholesale business with huge losses. Saved me from paying exorbitant sums of income tax from the sale of the newly acquired purchase. Steve was as good as his words. He sure knew how to sell. To unload the goods even quicker, I went to Germany I had a good client, a wholesaler in Hamburg. Through this client I got to know Gerhard. An able young man. Two years older than I. He had fought in Russia. One of the few lucky ones to have survived. As he said, *by train I was taken to the extreme south of the Ukraine. Back till Berlin, on foot.*

I spent a wonderful three weeks in Hamburg. With all the destruction, the atmosphere was a very happy one. Gone was the pressure of the deadly dictatorship. With Gerhard, a very jolly fellow, I spent the evenings at the top entertainment place, the Repperbahn. Sang and danced, saw cabarets, joined in the, then most popular song *wer soll das bezahlen, wer hat soviel Geld......*

Gerhard introduced me to a half a dozen of his friends. They thought I am German. No-one talked about the war. Like Gerhard, they had all fought on the Eastern Front. As arranged with Gerhard, he told them I am Jewish. The two girls came to embrace me and cried. The boys were pale. They soon found their composure and we continued in the same happy way. I didn't ask questions, nor did they. The war as though it never was. The enormous destruction, the only reminder.

Apart from our stock, manufacturers gave me their collections. Additional earning for Gerhard. I was sorry to leave, yet in Gerhard, I left behind an excellent and very reliable salesman. I had already extended my stay from the intended one week anyway.

A new business came my way. A Mr. Blechner, a neighbour of ours in Hampstead Gardens Suburbs asked me to find Army surplus goods, mainly blankets. The buyer of these goods was Eisenberg, who I knew from my refugee days in Japan. He married the daughter of a very wealthy Japanese family and stayed in Japan throughout the war. I understand in view of the influence of his father in-law, he must have been the only Jewish refugee not interned.

During my search for army  surplus auctions I landed in Newcastle. An opportunity to have dinner with a very good client, I had never seen before. The first day I had an opportunity to see the goods, laid out in numbered lots. The next day I went to the auction. There were mostly blankets, the item I was interested in. I won the bid for all of them. Gave a ten per cent check as a deposit and returned to the hotel. Very late in the evening I got a telephone call from the auctioneer. *I'm very sorry there has been a mistake you cannot have the goods please come by in the morning to get your cheque.* My first experience of favouritism or corruption or whatever it can be named, by a government organization.

## Chapter 13: The Net closes in.

Nineteen-fifty rolled into 1951. In December 1951, I went on a business trip to Brussels, as I did every couple of weeks. On a Saturday, I proceeded to the airport. The Sabena flight that I was about to board was delayed due to bad weather. When it arrived, I noted it had come in from Prague. For a split second I thought about letting that flight go, and getting another one the next day. But I was in a hurry to get home

There were some Czech nationals on the plane. I kept out of their way, kept my head buried in a book for the whole journey. When we disembarked in England, an immigration official pulled me aside.

*Wait a moment*, he said. He asked me to empty my pockets. I did so willingly, I had nothing to hide. I soon realized he was playing delay-action tactics. Only I was stopped. When he finally released me, late at night, there were no more Airport buses. I took a taxi home.

On Sunday morning I had a date with a girlfriend to have brunch together. As I drove through the comparatively empty streets of London, I soon suspected I was being followed. I took diversionary measures, darting down a side street, taking another side street, and then returning to the main street. Yes, there was the same car behind me. I picked up my friend and we drove out to the countryside to a pre-arranged restaurant. I kept my eyes on my rear-view mirror. There was always a car behind me. The cars were switched. There was too little traffic to fool me.

From that moment on, I was being followed all the time. I also suspected my telephone was being tapped. What was worrying me more than anything, I didn't know who was following me. The British, the Czechs or the Russians.

I had to find out. One day in the centre of town, in heavy traffic, I cut off my pursuer, jammed on my brakes, jumped out of the car and ran up to the car behind.

*What do you want?* I demanded. *Nothing.* He replied. *Then why are you following me. We're not,* was his answer.

There was a policeman nearby. I called him over and said, *These men are following me, I don't know who they are."*

The men in the car had a genuine English accents, but that didn't mean anything. One of them pulled the policeman aside and showed him some card or document. I couldn't see what it was. The policeman told me I was mistaken. So it was now obvious , it was the British. That is all I wanted to know.

Soon afterwards, I took Father out for a drive in the car and told him everything. He had no idea I was connected with Czech Intelligence. We discussed the possibility of my leaving England. I began to think about Argentina. When I first contacted their embassy I was in possession of a Czech passport. In the meantime I had applied for a British citizenship and they replaced my Czech passport with a laissez-passer.

I felt I had to do something, but what I did was the worst thing to do. I left a message for my emergency Czech contact, who I haven't seen after I asked him about rumours of changes in the Czech leadership. We arranged a meeting. I told him I was being followed. He assured me nothing drastic has changed in Prague and he was willing I should meet people in the leadership who I knew well, without actually specifying who he meant. There is only one way to meet them, I would have to come to Prague. He suggested I arrange a business trip to Vienna. From there I should proceed by train to Prague with a Czech passport that would be ready for me. I was too naïve to smell a rat. Or perhaps not so naïve. Not even the very able British Intelligence knew their bosses are Russian spies.

I did as he suggested, flew to Vienna at the end of February, checked in at the Ambassador hotel, that was still half destroyed, phoned a prospective business client and we arranged to meet. I took a taxi, and as we drove along, I noticed a sign: You are leaving the Allied Zone. At that time there was still a Russian zone in Vienna.

*Just a minute*, I said to the driver, *Is the address I gave you in the Russian zone?* He affirmed my suspicion. I asked him to stop and drive back to the hotel. Being in the situation where I was involved (however loosely) with Czech Intelligence, I was afraid to go into the Russian zone! When we arrived back to the hotel, I telephoned my business friend and told him I would be delighted to see him at my hotel the following morning.

I sat down for dinner. The waiter, assuming I am English broke his tongue with the few words he knew. I played his game. When it came to the last course I asked in German *haben Sie Dukaten Buchteln mit Vanille Krem?* He was flabbergasted yet produced a pleasant smile and brought me the dish I asked for. Never having been to Vienna before I went out for a walk, asked a young lady how to get to Grunzig, the entertainment place of Vienna. She was happy to accompany me there, showed me around and we ended up at a typical Viennese night club. The rest of the night I spent with her in another hotel. Returning to the Ambassador in the early morning I was told by the reception clerk somebody was here last night looking for me. He didn't leave a message.

Whilst I was having breakfast, a well-dressed gentleman came to see me. I invited him to join me for breakfast. He handed me a folded newspaper and told me there was an envelope with a passport in it. There also a train schedule and an emergency telephone number *in case you should be stopped at the border*. He asked me to buy some postcards and write them to my parents. He would post one every few days so they would not suspect I was no longer in Vienna.

Back in the room I had a look at my passport with my photo and in the name of Karel Valíček.

I boarded a fast direct train to Prague. On the Czech side of the border, an immigration official looked at my passport and ordered me to step down. He took me into an office and started firing questions at me. I did not answer any of them, I just gave him the phone number. *Ring this number*. As he spoke to the person at the other end, I saw his whole body language change. He stiffened as if he was standing to attention. I realized he must be speaking to someone very important. Someone he obviously knew.

Meanwhile the train was waiting. I didn't see anyone else getting off. The immigration officer accompanied me politely back to the train and off we went again.

In Prague I was met at the station and taken to a villa outside Prague. I was familiar only with the centre of the city. I wasn't sure exactly where I was. All I recognized was the Vyšehrad castle. At the villa they fired questions at me. They were horrified that I had never received any training.

I stayed for a week. It was very comfortable but I only saw the two interrogators. One day they drove me to the centre of town. They let me down in front of the Prašná Brána. I was told to wait for them to return. Should anyone I know approach me, I should tell them I live in Brno. I saw a few people, including a girl, a close acquaintance. To her question, why she did not see me for some time, the pre-arranged answer, I am in Brno now and she went her way.

It is only many years later that I understood this whole procedure. I started to worry for two reasons. I was not introduced to any government or communist official I knew. I also realized I had done something stupid by writing all those postcards to make my family think I was in Vienna. No one knew I was in Prague. I could just disappear.

The driver and the two interrogators took me back to the villa. Now I was very careful. I didn't ask questions. Never asked again nor mentioned the fact that I was not given a chance to speak to somebody I know. I only hoped I could return to Vienna in one piece. Greatly relieved, I was put on a train back to Vienna. There was no trouble at the border and I arrived safely back in England. I did not tell Father what had happened or where I had really been.

Before I left Prague I was given a day, time and place to meet with a contact. Here I would no longer be afraid to ask what my visit was all about. The purpose to speak to someone I knew and trusted was not even mentioned in Prague. I showed up as pre-arranged, a few steps from St. Paul cathedral. No-one came. I followed procedure, waited a few minutes, went away and returned half an hour later. No one there, I left. What could he have told me, *none of your friends had the time to meet you ?* I understood my visit had a purpose. Didn't know for a long time what it was all about.

Since then I lost all contact with the Czechs. I understood, that after the episode in Prague I could be of no use to them. The only thing that did not change, I was being followed.

As the media came out with the news of arrests of leading Communist leaders, culminating in the Slansky trial, I now understood why I couldn't meet anyone. All those I was acquainted with must have already been in jail. Why then was I asked to come to Prague ? Why then did they let me out again ? I was after all part of that group arrested and on trial!

## Chapter 14: Interlude

I considered leaving England. I was travelling to Europe all the time. I could easily have not returned from one of those trips. But how could I leave my parents. I had persuaded father to come back from Canada to be with me in the business. I knew he could not handle the business on his own. The company had grown much above the capacity he was used to. My father did come to the office nearly every day. Always with the same limousine, same driver, about 11am and left a couple of hours later.

I was all work, my only break was for lunch in one of the nearby restaurants. Had to stand in line to get a place at a table. Before I had a chance to swallow my last bite, the waitress came with the bill.

It was at one of these restaurants that the gentleman at my table mentioned he works at a nearby exporter, runs a department alone, does the buying and the selling and feels he should actually get a cut of the profit but doesn't. That's how I met Howard. I gave him my card and asked him to drop in for a chat. He did. He traded in Lever Lace. An article I have never heard of before. His suppliers in Nottingham, his clients in South America. His biggest client, a Jewish/German immigrant in Bolivia. As I later found out. We struck a deal. I let him have an office in our building, pay all expenses, do the financing and we split the gross profit 50/50. He was grateful for my generous offer. He was great. I gave the lace business a considerable push when I met a very interesting lady in Belgium, at one of my nylon stockings clients. Mrs. Laub, always in a mink coat, the same diamonds on her ring. bracelet, earrings, pendant. All a mere 6 karat! No doubt an excellent business woman. When she discovered I also deal in lace, she jumped of joy. She came over to London, discussed her requirements with Howard then with me the business procedure. I would deliver the goods to Switzerland, she would pay in Swiss francs. From Switzerland she had a way to get the goods to her clients in Spain. Spain did not give import licenses for such goods.

Sidney Lewis had or was connected with mills making cotton piece goods. He told me of a big demand in Pakistan. He could deliver the goods, the way the Pakistanis like, 25 yards packed in cellophane with a woman's picture covering one whole side. After inquiring and finding potential clients, I contacted Arnold Schlesinger. Arnold was a mechanic at my squadron, Henry's good friend. He came from Zilina, had studied at the Hebrew high school (gymnasium) in Munkačevo. The only Hebrew high school in Czechoslovakia. He visited me occasionally at my office. I proposed he should go to Karachi. I gave him the names of prospective buyers, who had already received my samples. Gave him the name of the biggest importer, to sell to him first, even at a lower price. Arnold liked my offer, made his way to

Karachi, settled in the finest hotel and soon started sending sizable orders. Sidney was very pleased.

In view of my contact with Pakistan, Riley bicycle makers made me one of their exporters to Pakistan, paying a 3% commission. My work was only documentation.

I continued with my usual routine. Went out with girls, theatre, concert, opera or just for dinner. Participated in meetings of various charity organizations to help Israel. To balls, mostly at Grosvenor House or the Dorchester hotel. I found the idea of all men dressed in smoking-jackets better than competing who wears the smartest suit. That competition was left to the young ladies. They had it good. An unwritten rule to go to the ball with a lady escort. One had to pick up the young lady with an orchid, which she pinned on her dress. One such evening was less successful. What we thought to be the very usual London fog, in fact was the first experience of the terrible smog. On the way to pick up my escort, I got stuck in the centre of London for hours. No cellular phone or other means of communication, I just left the car in the middle of the road, near Marble Arch, like everybody else and walked home. Only the next late morning did I succeed to get my car out.

I was convinced my *spy career* was at the end. They were leaving me alone. I guess I was lulled into a sense of false security. Had I thought otherwise I would have made different arrangements with the business.

In 1953, I visited Israel for the first time. I had several cousins who had settled in that country. The occasion, or excuse, was the bar mitzvah of Nizan Heruti, a cousin's son, who I didn't know. I decided this would be a good occasion to renew contact with the family I knew and get to know others I had never met. One of my cousins, Hanna, who grew up with us, was in Givat Chaim. Another, Ryvka, came to Palestine in the mid-1930s, right after visiting us in Teplitz. It is thanks to her that I have documents and photographs of my childhood. Teplice we left, in a more/less organized fashion. Our escape over the Polish border, was a different story. With nothing.

Another family, my mother's sister, emigrated to Palestine in 1925. They had a big family: four boys and two girls. Their youngest son, BenAmi, was born in Magdiel. The first child to be born in that new village. His brother Aaron served in the Palestine unit during WW2 and visited us in London during the war. Another brother, Elyakum fell in the war of Liberation. The same day as their mother passed away.

Before leaving England I needed clothes for the hot climate. Austin Reed, the prestigious menswear store in Regent street, had a tropical department. There I kitted myself out with shorts, short sleeve shirts etc., as advised by the sales people. To my surprise, at the still very colonial King David hotel, shorts were not the apparel to wear.

The flight took about twelve hours, in three stages London-Rome, Rome-Athens, Athens-Lud. Till Rome I sat alone, the two seats behind me were occupied by the famous cellist, Zara Nelsova. On the vacant seat, her cello. In Rome she moved to sit next to me and her cello was taken away, placed somewhere else, despite her protests. Though a Russian name she is English. Nelsova, to fit her profession. It was pleasant to have somebody to talk to. In Tel-Aviv I took her out for dinner and in turn she invited me to her concert she gave at the American Zionist House in Ibn Gvirol street. Shmuel, Hanna's husband joined me. Shmuel, also a great music lover, a native of Znojmo, Moravia. As though planned Nelsova played my favourite cello concerto by Dvořák.

As was most natural, I chose to fly with El Al. Back I flew with British Airways. Then El-Al stewardesses thought travellers enjoy rude behaviour. I didn't.

The cousin to meet me at the airport was the mother of the Bar Mitzwah boy and her husband, a taxi driver. Policeman under British rule. Took me to the hotel I had booked, the Kate Dan, supposedly the best Tel-Aviv hotel. Not very much impressed, I accepted my cousin's invitation to stay with them the first night. The only real good hotel I heard of, the King David in Jerusalem.

That's where I went by  taxi the next morning and stayed there for the rest of my fortnight's visit. Though an excellent hotel, I was surprised at the low price, $10.50 half board.

Based in Jerusalem, I hired a taxi to take me to see the country. Visited my relations, most often, Hanna and family in Givat Chaim. Her 12 year old son, Uzi, spoke some English. To my surprise with a Hungarian accent. His teacher was Hungarian.

I was very impressed with the country, had a comfortable feeling being in Israel. Obviously things looked rosy from a tourist perception. One thing I loved, seeing the blue sky and the constant sunshine. A rarity in London.

I found it very odd, that my cousin BenAmi, a farmer, couldn't get a permit to buy a tractor for his work. I sent him a tractor from England. I soon found that the whole economic system made no sense.

My visit had also a business nature. Together with a group of young entrepreneurs I was to initiate talks to establish a most modern inter-urban bus service. We knew about the dismal state of buses in Israel. No chance. Like practically everything else, it was Trade Union controlled. They owned practically everything. Together with the Socialist government they were strong enough to keep out competition.

Back in London I continued with the business which was expanding rapidly and becoming more profitable. Though Father could not be active in the business, it was good to have him to talk to, to discuss things, to share the decision-making. We discussed buying a house, as an investment. Father had more time. He came home one day, very happy. He bought a new, eight stories high apartment building. I was pleased. Not so pleased when a few days later he sold it for a few thousand pounds profit. I wanted an investment, not to deal in real estate.

Although I had no more contact with the Czechs, I was still being followed. I also knew that sometimes my telephone was tapped. Still thought about leaving, but loyalty to my parents prevented me doing anything about it. The Slánsky trial, the final confirmation, Czechoslovakia ceased to be a free country. I saw no reason for British Intelligence to suspect me now.

Could I have known that their treasonous bosses needed me as a Fall Guy ?

Parents wanted to see me married, so did I. I had many options.

Chose to get serious with Claudia Michaels.

Claudia's father was ill with lung cancer despite never having smoked. He was very fond of me, and as his health deteriorated he told me to look after his wife and daughter, just before he passed away. I admit I did feel somewhat pressured – both from him and my own parents.

The wedding was booked for the end of March 1954 at the Mayfair Hotel.

Everything was ready: clothes organized, invitations had been sent out. About two weeks before the wedding date, my parents and I were rudely awakened at about five o'clock in the morning by a heavy pounding on the apartment door. Not suspecting anything and not at all afraid, still in my pyjamas, I went to open the door.

## Chapter 15: Arrest and Deportation

Four men barged into the apartment and demanded to see me. First they searched me to check whether I had a suicide cyanide pill hidden somewhere. They then proceeded to search the apartment, opening cupboards, turning drawers upside down, looking under mattresses. A good ransacking. Probably disappointed that they didn't find anything, and I had not made a run for it or tried to jump out of a window, they took me into one of the rooms and started asking me questions.

I had nothing to hide. I couldn't give them some juicy facts Their main line of questioning was about the woman in Bradford. When they showed me her picture I recognized her as being the secretary of Zenkl, a right wing minister in the Czech government. I didn't deny it. They knew a lot about me. They knew my code name – Valsorim. They knew about my visit to Vienna and Prague. However, I felt quite confident. I naively thought, what can they do to me? I have done nothing wrong. I am in Britain, a democratic country.

I didn't know then, when it concerns intelligence, the democratic rule does not apply.

After I read Peter Wright's **Spy Catcher** I realized that it was all a set up using me to hide their treachery. Used me to cover their own behind. They had to show some results. With my past, it was easy to pick on me. My communist past, my position in Prague, activity at the British Czechoslovak Friendship league, living in a luxurious apartment at a prestigious address in central London, my fast financial ascent. Easy to claim they caught a big fish who financed the whole espionage ring in England. In the end they were satisfied to claim I informed on Czechs, living in England. They had to be careful not to exaggerate or the honest Intelligence people could smell a rat. They knew everything about me. They knew better than I did, that I had done nothing. The only service I ever did for Czech Intelligence was to bring Miss Schoenova the thirty pounds in cash. That was actually the first trick they played on me.

The only thing I denied was that I was a member of the communist party. I had left my party card with Osvald Zavodsky, who assured me that nobody could ever find proof of my party membership. I could have saved my breath. Osvald was by then already arrested, if not executed He was the only leading Czech communist executed in 1954, after the death of Beria.

The search of the apartment continued for two or three hours, then they left. Even at that point father and I discussed the possibility of my going away to Europe. But it was not feasible. Father could not cope with the business and it was not yet the computer, e-mail era when communication can be handled so easily and efficiently by remote control.

There was no immediate fall-out from that visit. Claudia and I continued with our wedding preparations. Two weeks later, two policemen arrived at my office at Finsbury Square to arrested me.

After Peter Wright's disclosures, I realized my visit to Prague at the beginning of 1952 was stage managed. The Czechs knew perfectly well they are not in a position to show me anyone I knew. At that time most of the top leadership of the communist party, those, who I knew, were already under investigation or in jail. Letting me stand in front of the Prašná Brána, what for? They asked me to stand there, then came to pick me up. Could have only be for one reason, an opportunity to take my photos at a well-known landmark in Prague. Obvious proof that I work for Czech Intelligence. And the young lady friend? Must have also been part of their game. She knew me too well, that one sentence, that I am now in Brno, made her walk away? Wouldn't she have asked what I am doing there? Why am I not in uniform? A game to convince a court in England or whichever authority that decided on my deportation. Also my meeting with a contact man after my Prague visit was arranged near St Paul's cathedral, an obvious London landmark. Probably the person to meet was a member of the Czech or Russian Embassy, standing somewhere near me, without my knowledge.

I was taken to Scotland Yard and the questioning started all over again. This time, compared to the previous officers, the interrogator was not as dumb. He went over and over with the same questions trying to catch me of inconsistency of my replies. The same questions over and over again. With this monotony he obviously tried to wear me out, exhaust me.

After many hours of interrogation I said I was thirsty. He asked someone to bring me a drink. It never came. I had my own back! Remembering instructions we got at the RAF in case we fall into the hands of the Germans. At interrogations keep on looking at the interrogators shoes and do so from side to side, as though you see something. It worked. At first he tried to see what I am looking at. He went out, came back. I looked the other way. No doubt he felt uncomfortable, even nervous. Maybe he would have kept on drilling me. Eight to ten hours without food or drink, quite enough. He innocently thought he can get something out of me. Like me, he didn't know his bosses are the spies. I had no watch. He must have had a bite and drink the many times he left the room.

In jail I was in solitary confinement. Nothing, but an iron bed. No water basin or lavatory. In case of need, had to bang for quite some time and escorted there and back. I refused to eat the uneatable food. At my expense I had food brought in from a restaurant. Whoever had selected my food supplier, did a good job.

After a couple of days I was taken from jail to be drilled again, this time by a senior officer, for a change a very pleasant guy. I was now completely open with him. Look, I understand you know everything and you also know I didn't do a thing. I am totally against the Russian system. This is the reason I left the Czech Air Force and left Czechoslovakia. All my old friends in Czechoslovakia have either disappeared or are in jail or even executed. The Czechoslovakia I knew and wanted to help after the end of the war, does not exist anymore. I am the last to help a Russian controlled Czechoslovakia. Again, he is not to blame. He must have thought I keep some great secrets he wants me to confess to. The fact that they found nothing in my apartment. Discovered nothing following me two years long. Not innocent, just very clever!

After the many hours with the senior officer, they took me back to Brixton prison.

I could not believe this was happening. I went through all the interrogation procedures as if in a dream. As I heard the metal doors clanging behind me I thought I was viewing a film.

Solitary confinement with no access to the outside world, no phone calls to family, no contact with a lawyer. Never mind laws governing incarceration. Where Intelligence is involved, no laws seem to count.

When father finally discovered I was in jail, he considered to apply to the Lord Chief Justice, Lord Shawcross, for *Habeas Corpus*. (The right of someone in prison to appear in a court of law, so the court can decide whether that person should stay in prison or protection for an unlimited imprisonment without charges). Two lawyers appeared in my cell. By their questions, I soon realized they were plants by Intelligence. They were trying to find out things, trying to trick me. Again there was nothing to trick me about. Who had hired them ? Why did our lawyer Mr Tarlo not come ?

The two lawyers' advise at the end of the long talk: Habeas Corpus costs 1,000 pounds per day, and there is no knowing how long it will take before you get a court appearance. Whether you are guilty or not, is irrelevant. If they want to prove something against you, they will, including producing witnesses etc. Now I know the reason they didn't want me to be in court. Hearing my testimony, some decent Intelligent Officers could have understood my trip to Prague was not in the Czechs' interest. There was already sufficient suspicion of treason high up. The ease of Maclean and Burgess slipping out proved it. The planted lawyers held a red herring before me. They want to send you back to Czechoslovakia. We will fight against it. In Czechoslovakia your life will be in danger. I didn't yet know or suspect that the Czechs are the ones, who threw me to the dogs. I didn't understand the whole game. What I did know that all I was in contact with, are no more. Executed or jailed. Jailed were also those who had served in the British Air Force and British Army during WW2. The country was under Russian rule. The basis; political terror. Over the radio I heard, how Andre Simone, chief editor of the Rude Pravo was questioned. It was the 1936 trials in Moscow all over again. Andre Simone was one of a group of middle-aged communists who spent the Second World War in Mexico. I visited him in Prague very often. He was an absolute mine of information; he was my encyclopaedia. It was heart-breaking to hear him admit that he worked against socialist Czechoslovakia.

At first I was defiant and challenged the lawyers –tell them to charge me.

Don't waste your time and money, if they charge you, you will lose.

Finally father got permission to visit me. He could not actually come into my cell like the lawyers. I had to use a cubicle with very heavy glass and the talk was with earphones on both sides. With father I agreed to accept the lawyers idea not to ask for habeas corpus. I actually knew they didn't have to take me to court. My visa of residence had a stipulation, that the Home office had the right to cancel it. Didn't have to give a reason.

The question now, which country to choose. All embassies of European countries father approached did not object to receive me, so I had many options. I would have indeed chosen a European country, particularly one we had business contacts with. That would have been my decision, had I not been to Israel the year before. I therefore decided for Israel. As it worked out it was the worst decision.

The lawyers succeeded to get the authorities to agree that I could go to a country of my choice. Israel was not overjoyed to receive me. Officials from the Israeli embassy visited me in jail. They were admitted to my cell. Though not sure if I'm telling them the truth, they understood I would hardly be safe to return to Czechoslovakia. The 1952 purge actually removed all Jews from the Party leadership. It was no secret that I was in close contact with most of them.

Whilst the legal negotiations were going on, weeks passed. I read a lot, almost a book a day. I read all three volumes of Somerset Maugham's short stories. I read a lot of detective stories, books of a type I never touched before.

Though in solitary confinement, I had contact with two other prisoners. One a Polish thief in a cell very near mine. Whenever permitted to leave my cell, I played chess with him. He told me the way he worked. He entered homes only in the mid mornings after he saw the housewife leave. No problem getting into the house through the main door with a self-constructed universal key. Took only money, jewellery and small items he could put in his pockets. He was never caught, a fence gave him away. He was intelligent, spoke good English. To my question, why not go straight. *And work a full day for a fraction of the money I make now*? He said he learned his lesson and will only steal money. Fences are known to the police. Another prisoner I befriended was during the daily walk in the courtyard. A Pakistani involved in arms smuggling. I had read about him in the paper. He was caught shipping arms to Poland. The only daily exercise we had was walking in line in the courtyard. During the walk I chatted with him. Warders always interrupted our conversation. He promised to be in touch with me, when free again. Needless to say I never heard from him.

And then it was Pesach, and a rabbi conducted a Seder for the Jewish prisoners. There were less than a dozen of us. That was the most interesting Seder night I ever attended, in the company of thieves and crooks! It was also very sad for me. I remembered with nostalgia, the Seder nights from my childhood, a very important festival in our home. I tried to recall the tunes father used but couldn't. The war years had erased some of those childhood memories.

Soon after Pesach, the news came through. I could go to Israel! As I was later told, the help came from the Haganah people, who visited me at Air Force Headquarters in Prague in 1947. I had no way to check if this was true or not.

The whole story was splattered all over the British press, but not only the British papers. All over the world. Friends and relatives from Argentina and Uruguay phoned parents. They had read the story in their papers. Things moved very quickly after that. I wanted to get married before going. Father tried to dissuade me, he felt it would be better if I went alone. I should have listened to him.

I needed to buy things for Israel and for the wedding. They allowed me to leave jail for a few days for shopping and other errands. I left jail each morning with two escorts, and back to jail at the end of the day. These escorts were with me wherever I went, also to the shops where I did my purchases.

We cancelled our big wedding, only a few days before the due date. My sister and her sons had already arrived from Canada. My cousin, Shimon, who I had found in Paris, after its liberation in 1944, also came.

Claudia and I had a brief wedding ceremony at her mother's home, which, although officiated by a rabbi, was not recognized as kosher in Israel, and we had to have an additional ceremony there. The introduction to idiotic laws in Israel. Apart from my two escorts, there were two surprise visitors attending the wedding who I didn't know.

Don't you remember us? We visited you at the Air Force Headquarters in Prague in 1947. One was Nissan Shapira from Tel-Aviv, with whom I became later very friendly. The other was from Haifa, who I visited later a couple of times.

Some time in 1947, the Czechoslovak Air Force Chief rang me, wanted to talk to me. I intended to come to his office. We were on the same floor. He preferred to come to me. The first time ever. Told me your people are here. I didn't understand what he meant till he told me Haganah representatives from Palestine. They are asking for the use of an airport. I didn't think much and suggested Zatec, a well-equipped airport, seldom used. To my question, if he would agree to such an arrangement, his answer was positive. *But you see to it that I get the O.K. from the highest quarters,* he said. Back at his office, he called me again. *Two of the Haganah people want to meet you.* These were the two, who had now come to my private wedding. I saw them for too short a moment to remember, what they look like.

I was very interested the Haganah should indeed get the use of the Czech airport. I turned to the one man who could do it; even get the prime minister's approval.

Bedřich Rajcín, head of Army Inteligence. (Later also deputy Minister of War. One of the 13 executed after the Slánský trial in 1952).

After the wedding I went back to jail, and a day or two later was escorted from jail to the airport. Claudia joined me as I boarded the plane. The first leg of the journey was to Rome. My escorts were still with me. When we changed planes in Rome, I took my leave of my British jailers.

From Rome, we travelled to Athens and then on to Lod airport. As we disembarked, another surprise awaited us. Reporters! I did not realize how much my episode was followed in the Israeli press.

## Chapter 16: A new life in    Israel.

The first few days were a blur. We checked in at the Dan Hotel. A surprise look by the receptionist, when I gave Kibbutz Givat Chaim as my home address. A mounted policeman was on guard outside the hotel. For me or always there? No idea. I was besieged by reporters. I remember a comment written by one of the Yediot Aharonot reporters: *how can we expect to have good relations with the USA when we admit such a person.*

One of my friends from LSE, Val Sherman, had come to live in Israel and was a freelance writer. Later, he worked for the newspaper Ha'aretz. When I arrived he introduced me to Ze'ev Lacquer, a well-known historian, who gave me some useful advice, how to handle the press.

Claudia and I stayed at the Dan Hotel for some time. After a while the press lost interest in me and I had to decide what to do. I was approached by a number of people with various ideas, to buy certain businesses, to invest in existing enterprises. I investigated some of the offers. When I saw an advert by Ata, then the biggest textile outfit, looking for an export manager, I was eager to apply. When I told father about it *don't be employed by any-one, you have enough money to set up your own concern.*

I had an offer by an insurance company, by an investment bank, a Jerusalem printer to make playing cards. The first idea I decided to work on; to set up an inland airline. It was a Dutch pilot of El-Al who approached me. He spoke on behalf of a group of pilots. They wanted to set up an airline, utilizing the airport of Mahanayim. They had spoken to a number of kibutzim in the north who were very enthusiastic for such a plan to be realized. The pilots needed someone to push their program through. Find suitable planes, the financing and most off all, get the project approved by the government authorities. I needed a good lawyer. I chose Mr Braude, regarded one of the best. This lawyer got me top financial advisers, who had to work out the profitability of the project. Though profitability was an important factor for me, the authorities insisted to see it. Their excuse, to protect the investor, he shouldn't go into something unprofitable. **As though the socialists worried very much if a bourgeois was to lose money!** It didn't take me long to get an offer from England of six airplanes suitable for that task. Negotiations were with the director of the Ministry of Transportation. Numerous meetings, some with the lawyer, with the financial people. I was in all of these. Every time new papers, new information. Even got them letters from all the northern kibbutzim, how many flights a week they would require with how many people and at what price. At long last I was told the project would be examined and we'll let you know. They never did. Numerous days I phoned, I went myself to the ministry. I already knew the number of tiles to the office leading to the *All Mighty*,   till one day I was told, the director of the ministry had left for the USA for good. I consulted my lawyer, he investigated. His final answer, there is no use pursuing the matter any further.

I have no proof, just a suspicion that Arkia was based on my plan.

It was Dr. Kohlberg, had a pharmacy in Allenby and was head of the Pharmaceutical Association, who introduced me to a number of pharmaceutical factories and importers of chemicals. Of all those I spoke to I was most interested in Teva. Mr. Friedlander, owner of Teva, suggested I take over sales and requested $ 80,000. Then just 20,000 English pounds. The London business had liquid assets of more than 200,000 pounds. Although I had brought some money with me and had some at the Julius Baer bank in Zurich, it wasn't enough. When I asked my father to send me the money I needed, he sent $ 15,000 and that took long to arrive. That was a terrible shock. I could not possibly imagine what had happened.

It was the day after the Swiss bank informed me about the transfer that I opened the door at 6am and two men barged in. They banged so hard, they woke the whole house. I then lived in the Beit Hakerem part of Jerusalem. On the same floor, the door opposite lived Michael Ben Chanan, known for the daily morning radio exercise instructions. They started upsetting everything, spoke loudly, practically shouted. I had no idea what they are saying, till I thought one of  them has a Slav accent. *I am from Slovakia* he answered in reply to my question, where he came from. Now I could communicate. Where did you hide the 15,000 dollars. I thought this was a joke. It wasn't. Now I understood what this comedy was all about. I laughed. The money is in the bank. It was too early in the morning for the bank. Claudia made coffee for all of us, then I drove with the two jokers to the Union Bank in the centre of Jerusalem. We three entered the Bank manager's office and the senior of the Sherlock Holmes asked Mr Greenwald,the manager to be shown the 15,000 dollar transfer. The bank manager, very quietly and politely answered no problem at all then turned to me: *I can show your account to these gentlemen, providing you give me your **written** instructions to do so*. He stressed the word written. I caught on. Turned to my two escorts *go to hell* in English and in Czech in an even less polite version. At least one of them should understand.

Eric Lucas looked after the interests of the immigrants from England. It is thanks to him that I bought a one and a half dunam plot in Herzliya Pituach. My plan to build two homes there, one for myself and one for my brother. An architect, recommended by Eric, finished the plans for both houses. I was negotiating a five dunam plot in Savyon for agricultural purposes with the right to build one house there. Planned of having my cousin BenAmi handle the agricultural part. Now I put everything on hold.

Eric meant well. He set up an appointment for me with a high Air Force officer. Very pleasant talk. About the Israeli war of Liberation, WW2, my post-war Air Force activity. I made clear I have no intention of becoming again a professional soldier but I am just 32 and will have to serve in the reserve army, what rank, what job ? *You are overqualified, this is the problem*. I have heard this sentence before and it always followed with a negative sentence. He didn't think there is another Air Force navigator with my experience in Israel. *I understand you are a New Immigrant*. No I said, my present status, a temporary resident. I could see he loved my answer, I presented him with an escape hatch. *There is no use talking about it now, once you become Israeli, you apply through the normal channels and your case will be considered*. I didn't guess then. When a few years later I did become a New Immigrant and applied. I got the answer. Private, no rank. And why did I not agree to become a New Immigrant straight away? People, who knew, told me I would be no longer able to transfer money freely. For every transaction I would require a permit and run to get it from the corrupt administrators. This much I already experienced.

I knew all along, father was not able to deal with the business, the reason I didn't consider leaving England.

That he would be completely incapable of at least keeping it up and go ahead with our plan to liquidate and turn all into cash, I did not consider.

I thought up an alternative. To ask the Ministry of Trade and Industry to grant me an import license for worsteds for the value of 100,000 English Pounds (400,000 US dollars). I needed a contact a *macher*, not just myself approach the Minister. Actually the director of the Ministry of Trade and Industry. This I already knew. I was introduced to a high official of the General Zionists, the party running the Ministry of Trade and Industry. I met Shlomo Valero, I explained to him my predicament. He was no Socialist, himself a business man. I explained that due to English currency restrictions I cannot just transfer money to Israel. To bring goods is the easiest alternative. I suggested all the goods would go to a bonded warehouse. Not one meter would reach the local market. I would export all to my clients in Europe, USA, Canada. Foreign currency for Israel !! All the money I would invest in Israel.

A few days later I met the *macher* again. This time, at his request, at café Vienna. You can get an import license for only100,000 dollars, but you would be permitted to sell the goods on the local market. I was stunned by the generosity. Before I jumped out with my o.k., came the catch: I want first 10,000 dollars in cash. If I were not that young, on the spot, I could have got a heart attack. I calmed down and agreed ! To make sure I am not taken for a ride, I suggested. You will get the Bill of Lading for same goods. This we can arrange with the Clearing Agent, and you hand it over to me after getting your 10,000 dollars. He did not agree, wanted the money straight away.

I had kept father informed about my plan. When I told him I cannot get an import license, he laughed. Israelis are selling import licenses here in London.

I needed a car. I asked father to send me one. The only one I knew being imported in Israel, was the Vauxhall. As a temporary residence, I didn't have to pay duty. The procedure took very long, therefore I also ordered the only freely imported car, the Willis, from the USA. Just one person was permitted to import. How socialists love monopolies ! To buy a car from Ilin, one had to go through Mr. Goldman. $ 1,000 in cash with the order. Futile to ask if I'll get a receipt, had already been introduced to the black economy in England.

Nissan came with a new business opportunity. He was head of an organization called MFI (Materials for Israel). Connected with the USA only. Clothing manufacturers, with stock left over at the end of the season were asked to donate these goods to Israel. MFI organized it all, collected the goods, packed them and shipped them to Israel. Shekem received these goods to sell and give the proceeds to charitable organizations. Nissan was Head of

MFI. He told me of a shipment of men's trousers that had just arrived. He set up a meeting with Shekem's big boss for me. I entered the spacious office in Jaffa and was given the price per trouser, 16 Liras. Very reasonable. Then again a hitch. I would get an invoice for 6 Lira and 10 the big boss wanted in cash for himself. I thought I don't hear well. Then it sank in, it was real. When a business man makes such an offer, the goods are his. He is avoiding to pay income tax on the higher price. These goods were not his. He was stealing them from a charitable organization. I told him just that. So what ! He sold these trousers anyway and to a person, who by chance I knew. This buyer thanked me for not making the purchase.

This was too much. I went to see Michael Comay, Claudia's uncle. Michael was director of the Ministry of Foreign affairs. I told him what happened. Who can I complain to ? His answer: *All you can do, is to shut up, if you don't want to be arrested.* I heard it loud and clear. He was right, what chance have I got. Shekem's boss, an important Mapainik will deny it. Why should they believe me ? This is the system and those running it are untouchable. Just very recently I heard over the radio a commentator asking the previous lady State Controller, if there was less corruption before. She answered, that **before only the one giving the bribe could be prosecuted, never the one who took the bribe**. So Michael was right.

It hit me, how stupid, thoughtless I had been. With ease I could have prepared for myself a base in Switzerland, Belgium, Germany. I had $ 80,000 in a London safe, why not in another country ? I was making money, had a good time, every few weeks on the Continent. Even now, after this episode, it was not too late to rescue at least part of my assets. Become a New Immigrant, get an Israeli passport, go to Belgium, Germany, get import licenses there. Jeanette knew the export procedure. She had done that for the last five years. She knew the English forwarders, who could ship the goods. Parents would return to Canada, Claudia to England, till I set up a home in Europe. The valuable furniture, the Persian carpets could be shipped to Canada, for parent's home, so could the 50 paintings (Father got these from a client who couldn't pay his debt of some 10,000 pounds). The sale of the lease of the Portland Place apartment and the Finsbury building could be handled by Mr.Tarlo, our lawyer. A drastic step.

I didn't do it. Had I lost my *Durchschlagskraft*, my will to do things ? Taking chances? Had I prepared an alternative place in Europe, I surely would have gone ahead. Now, it meant going to another unknown place. One experience in a new country was more than enough. Before I could make up my mind, Nissan came with more propositions. Like one, to participate in Army car auctions, which I would always win and similar ones. I dismissed them all.

Nissan was married to Sima, one of the Kirpichnikov daughters. The Kirpichnikovs had the biggest store of fabrics in Nachlat Benyamin, Tel-Aviv. Sima's sister, Nechama was married to the well-respected Mr. Nattenberg, of Italian origin. Mr Nattenberg had joined Hans Heilig in a factory making fine men's suits for export. Some of these suits they exported, but most of them sold on the local market. This unlawful act landed them in jail. Nissan introduced me to the manager of Feuchtwanger bank, who not wanting to lose invested money, was looking for someone to mind the factory in the few months absence of the two partners. Two attractions, I would be introduced to the business world and it was in Jerusalem.

Claudia became pregnant the first month in the country, but it soon became apparent that our marriage was not working. She was a girl from a prosperous London suburb. The Middle East was not for her. Why did she go ahead with our marriage? I told her a number of times I would understand if she wished to pull out. In those few weeks, things were happening too quickly, that I am sure, like me, she could not think straight. She enjoyed being in the news. One thing she couldn't take, the humidity in Tel-Aviv. Jerusalem therefore, was a welcome alternative. We got both cars practically at the same time. Claudia used the Vauxhaul, I the Willis. Claudia did a good service to the two ladies, Nechama Nattenberg and

Shula Heilig, taking them to visit their husbands at the less strict Massiahu jail in Ramle.

We were both well received by the Jerusalem old timers. Judge Manny, lawyer Kaspi, the bakery owners Angel and Berman, the Schors, a Hadassa doctor who lived at the same building as Nechama, the Chazanovkis. We played tennis at the YMCA, played squash, went swimming to Shoresh. The social life was above all expectations and we were in a Jewish State.

Claudia went to England many months before the due date. Those months, she wanted to be with her mother and give birth at a hospital she knew.

Parents came to visit and together with Hanna I took them for a week to the Dolphin House in Shave Zion, near Nahariya. Pleasant atmosphere, Freddy Dura entertained in German and English. There I met Paul Pick, manager of the Orgil hotel in Jerusalem and agreed to stay in his hotel during the long months that Claudia was to spend in London. Menachem Begin was a weekly visitor, when the Knesset was in session. Quite a number of times we had breakfast together.

Heilig's factory was in an industrial building in Mekor Baruch. The factory was well organized, small overheads. Apart of one secretary, all were part of the production process. The factory manager was at the same time quality controller. The warehouse head, apart from seeing to it that required   fabrics and accessories are available, also packed the export goods in specially designed cartons. Exceptional and very hard working, was the works manager Albert Ohana, who, with a large family lived in the slums of Musrara. Overlooking the financial side of the concern was only part of my activity. I also visited local clients all over the country to receive orders and collect payment. Not, like in England, where clients sent the cheques at due dates. I was introduced to the world of post-dated cheques, and long-term bills.

The bureaucracy in England was bad, here it was idiotic. To export clothing, had to apply for an **export** license. If that was not enough, before every week's shipment an inspector came, quasi as quality controller. He named the village, where he was a tailor. His function to get a suit, sometimes demanded two. I didn't yet understand the need for two sets of cutting patterns for each style, for each size, one of which was never used. When an army of **know it all** experts entered and the correct patterns disappeared, I understood. Very seriously these pencil pushers placed these fake patterns on the cloth opened for them on the cutting tables, measured exactly how much cloth is needed for each item and at each size. Didn't leave out the smallest items. Dictated the result to their colleague, who knew how to write, in a loud and firm voice. Stamped and signed each pattern. Didn't leave out the date of inspection. The cloth was removed, came the linings, then the inter-lining, then the felt below the collars, even the loops on  the trousers. They were very efficient, didn't omit anything. Took a rest to smoke a cigarette and we served them Turkish coffee. Four hours, before they marched out. Showed the hated bourgeois who is the boss !

I was invited to a meeting of foreign investors. Sapir, the minister of Trade and Industry or Finance disclosed the newest plan; to build Dimona. Clothing was one of the industries needed there. He spoke in English. When Sapir asked *what can we do for you, to increase export*, I was the first to jump up. *Do nothing*, I told the minister. *Why should I need an export license, why a quality controller for clothing ? My controller is my client !* No! The minister didn't have to answer. Representatives of the big concerns, of the monopolies, answered for him: *Must have controls, can't let every Dick, Tom and Harry export and spoil Israel's name.* In other words, throttle competition.

Heilig and Nattenberg finished their time. Not being able to run the factory as before, they didn't have the money to continue. I took over. Nattenberg stayed for export sales. Heilig opened a retail shop. We supplied high quality cashmere coats to Grieder in Zurich, fine worsted suits to the leading men's stores in Zurich, Basel, Geneve. Increased sales on the local market.

Received also orders from     leading London stores. The salesman Claudia engaged during one of her London visits.

Claudia returned from England when Michael was nearly 4 months old. I did not know if she would return at all. She came with an English nanny. In addition to the nanny, we employed a daily maid, a cook and a woman who came in a couple of times a week to do the ironing. Our expenses were extremely high.

Henry came for a visit, just after the Sinai war in 1956. To him it was rather odd, so was it to me at first, whenever I parked the car, screwed off the aerial and took off the windscreen wipers. The wheels were less of a collectors' item! I intended to go with Henry to Sinai, but Israeli troops were already moving out. That BenGurion claimed not to withdraw without a peace agreement at a huge demonstration in Jerusalem, a lie to pacify the demonstrators.

Father visited me a few times. On the subject of liquidating the London business, he is making arrangements.

In June 1957 whilst Claudia was in England, my father passed away. I asked permission from the British authorities to go to England for the funeral and to liquidate the business. I even offered to pay for two escorts to accompany me   during the time of my stay. Nothing doing.

Father did not even start with our plan to liquidate as quickly as possible. He didn't listen to me or better said was not able to fulfil such a task. When he passed away the business was still there. I wanted Henry to go to England to liquidate. After all he ran it before I took over. My sister rushed to England before Henry could arrange leaving his work. Steffi liquidated the company very quickly. She had no idea how to go about it. She left a lot of assets behind, not aware of their existence, still collected a reasonable sum. All for herself.

In the early part of 1958, Claudia left for England with our son Michael. Our marriage was over. My loss, not to have contact with my son. 1968 I found a way to go to England. By chance Arnold's son went to the same school as Michael. This is the same Arnold Schlesinger, now Scott, who went for me to Karachi some years ago. Easy to get in touch with Michael. After seeing him I took the first available flight to the Continent. I correctly assumed my dear ex-wife would contact police.

I introduced a new idea; duty-free sales. The army of diplomats became my clients. Also members of the Czechoslovak Embassy. Got very friendly with the son of the Guatemala Ambassador, Gorges Granados. His father was expelled from England about the same time as I, having stated British Honduras is part of Guatemala. I played tennis and squash  with the young Granados at the YMCA. He became Ambassador after his father left. Gorges married an Israeli girl, who much later was in Israel as the Ambassador of Guatemala. Gorges had already passed away. I went to many diplomatic parties, as well as a X-mas party at Government House, then on the Jordanian side. This visit and a long conversation I had with the Czech Ambassador at one of the parties interested Mr. Leshem of our ministry of Foreign Affairs. This was the same gentleman who in 1955 suggested I should work for Israeli Intelligence and go to Paris. I was told Czechoslovakia is supplying arms to Egypt. I was not interested. He then asked if I could analyse reports from the Czech press. I would get Czech newspapers on a daily basis. To this I agreed. Never got a single newspaper.

The factory was doing well, the constant interference of officials from the Histadrut was unpleasant. *If you unionize, we can arrange a big loan on preferential terms.* That they also want 51% of the shares, just a bagatelle. They encouraged the girl workers to ask frequently for sick leave. I spoke to the doctor, why he gives them three days off for nothing. *I cannot take the risk, perhaps it is real.*

The factory had a name for high-class ready-made clothing. Also being in Jerusalem had an advantage. Not for me, because for the smallest requirements, Tel-Aviv was the place. Out of the blue, without even a prior telephone call, Mr Cecil Gee paid me a visit. Didn't know him personally, but I used to supply him with fabrics in London. I knew his shop in Golders Green. When he told me why he came to see me, it made me laugh. He wanted me to produce for him **kosher** suits. I had never heard of anything being kosher, but food. After a lecture which yarns and fabrics may not be mixed I knew there is no obstacle to produce such garments.

Next Cecil wanted on each garment an attractive embroidered label **Made in Jerusalem** and certified by the Jerusalem Rabbinate. The person I spoke to at the rabbinate was very helpful and in no time a representative came to the factory. In the meantime I had already inquired about the price of such labels from Tietz, a factory in Bnei Braq, the only one making embroidered labels. I did all quite openly in Cecil's presence. These were after all expenses not connected with the production process. I held myself not to fall off the chair, when this rabbinate representative not only stated, **he** will have to order these labels from the same factory but quoted a **ten times** higher price. That was only the beginning. For every suit I supply Cecil Gee, I have to pay the rabbinate 5 dollars. This is on a 25/30 dollar suit. Then there must be a rabbinate controller in the factory. I told him, *I can't have anyone roaming around in the factory. 'He won't disturb you, just make periodical checks outside working hours'.* Next came the demand for a monthly salary for same controller. The result, both Cecil Gee and I have had enough. I invited Cecil to a good oriental meal in Ben Yehuda Street to counter the unbelievable experience.

Henry sent me a sample of a new Canadian light weight fabric, Orlon. I consulted Yano Freund, an excellent designer and his wife Olga, leading Jerusalem dress maker. They thought it very suitable for ladies' coats for the European spring. I ordered enough fabric for a collection in four pastel shades. The Freunds made five models. The buyer of Harrods of London was very enthusiastic. Rang me and asked if the coats can be ready for the spring season. There was plenty of time and I was sure it can be done easily. The buyer knew me well and took my word for it. Harrods put the coat, no less, than on the **cover** page of the new spring collection brochure. At Dickens and Jones only my two Orlon coats in one of their big show windows.

I ordered enough fabric for orders in hand and a decent reserve for quick re-orders. I also made sure all previous orders to be finished in time and workers can go full speed ahead with the Orlon coats, as soon as the fabric arrives.

As the shipment arrived in Haifa, I asked the clearing agent to make an extra effort to get the goods to Jerusalem with utmost speed. Then the theatre started. I understood Customs in Haifa were in no hurry. I drove there to speak to the big boss, Mr Ellenberg. Wasted effort. He insisted all the goods must be opened, spread on the *very clean* warehouse floor, to attach heavy lead seals every meter with a string. This was to make sure I don't sell the fabric on the local market.

I showed Mr.Ellenberg orders from Harrods and other leading British shops for the whole imported quantity. The loss not only for me, the trade reliability of Israel manufacturers. I suppose he heard of England but Harrods to him sounded like another trick invented by the capitalistic cheat out to harm the very State of Israel. Talk to a brick wall. Mr. Ellenberg was true to his word, just as he said, after three weeks I got the goods. Three weeks 40 workers sat idly in the factory and I paid them full wages.

In the late afternoon, the last of the Orlon goods were unloaded. The cutter, work manager, store keeper and myself worked till late at night to make sure the workers had their bundles ready at their machines for the next morning. We could still manage to deliver the coats on time.

Then the bombshell. None of the workers turned up in the morning. I asked Albert to find out what happened. Like Albert, all the workers were new immigrants from Morocco. They were threatened by the Trade Union not to dare work for me, unless I agree to be unionized. I was the last one to give in to blackmail. The seamstresses cried, begged the sort-off  workers representatives to let them go back to work. In the end they won the battle - but they lost the war. Three weeks later they all showed up. We produced and sent as much as we could before the target date. The rest of the orders were cancelled. My name was deleted from the suppliers' list. I telephoned, I pleaded, told them what happened. The answer was the same from every client. *We are not interested why, just the fact, that you are not in a position to deliver on time.*

A big American outfit contacted me to fully employ the factory on a yearly basis. Fine quality men's pants. They supply the fabrics, the linings and all other accessories. I was no longer interested to fight this idiotic administration. I contacted the Stopper brothers, also in Jerusalem. They accepted. They were after all old-timers. Knew better how to handle the self- important, good-for-nothing officials. They spoke their language. I didn't speak any Hebrew. Later the Rapaports took over. Also used their weaving plant to produce the fabric for the pants.

Rosenblum begged me to sell him all the Orlon. He still owed me a considerable sum from previous purchases. His excuse, he invested a lot of money in a much bigger shop. For him it was natural, to use my money to get himself a shop. I also didn't need another headache to sell goods on the local market, that were earmarked for export. I closed the factory, paid the workers, also for the weeks they were on strike. I let my lawyer handle the liquidation. The government took me to court for owing some enormous sum. Before any hearing, the authorities confiscated all goods and machinery. Even a metal suitcase, that I had kept in the factory. Though it contained just books but also a most important item, my log book of all of my 49 operational missions as navigator during the war. I asked a number of times to let me have this box back. In the end I made a written request. You have already received it, was the answer.

At the lawyer's advice I sold my one and a half dunam plot in Herzlia-Pituach. In the early morning of the day of the first hearing in court, my lawyer died of a heart attack. He was in the early forties.

The law office of Mr Kollek, cousin of Teddy Kollek, took my case. He gave my file to one of his young lawyers, who asked for a postponement to study the file. This lawyer meant well, but didn't know enough. Wasn't witness of the run-around I suffered from the Socialist do-gooders. My lawyer showed a document from the Ministry of Trade and Industry, that I owe 2,300 Israeli Pounds, about US$ 1,000.- purchase tax for goods I had bought from local manufacturers. That payment was not even due yet. Just the statement, without any documentation by the government lawyer that this 1,000 dollar demand was a mistake, was enough for the judge to accept. *The good old Ben Gurion days*. I saw my young lawyer to suddenly    perspire. I was afraid, he too, is about to get a heart attack. Now came new demands. Duty and purchase tax for the goods, they had confiscated. I suggested to let me sell the goods and I can pay it all. How naïve. They wanted to sell them.

I left Jerusalem, went to stay with an aunt in a half room of her poor small ground floor apartment in the southern part of Hayarkon Street. Her husband, deceased, was my mother's brother. They had lived in Leipzig in luxury. Came to Palestine, in the early fifties. Since 1953, I supported them.

I brought a small suitcase with just a few items of my huge garde-robe, I had come to Israel with. Now I was homeless. Thinking back, I must be made of steel, not having entertained, not even for a moment, to end my life. My only solution, to leave the country.

Albert came to see me. He wants to continue making high class suits for the local market. I should help him to get orders. He'll work only with home workers, all who had worked in the factory. I still had my Vauxhall, the Willis I had sold when Claudia left.

I decided to go to Germany. I was in touch with Nissan, he had just settled there. I changed my status to: New Immigrant, applied for a passport. The sale of my car would pay for my fare. I now only waited to get my Israeli passport.

Small incidents can change   one's life ! I met Sally. She was with a lady acquaintance. Sally, a beautiful woman, was one of the ladies Claudia played cards with in Jerusalem. After Claudia left, I had a short romance with her. She wanted me to meet her again. She is now staying with her parents in Tel-Aviv. She left her husband. Her parents bought her the apartment in Jerusalem. She can't ask for it, as her daughter, aged six stayed with her father. We met a few times. Sally wanted that we marry. With what ? I am penniless, homeless. Her answer: *You'll work yourself up again !* Very optimistic indeed. Anyway, we were both not divorced.

I kept on working with Albert. Sally got her divorce, I got my divorce. We married Feb 1, 1960 in a small hall. The food was supplied by friends and relations. Rented a one room apartment in Givatayim.

Dr. Stern, a casual acquaintance wanted to see me. Kibbutz Neve Eitan in Emek Beith Shan took over a factory producing Army trousers. They needed some-one to run it for them. I went to see the place. The factory was in Beth Shan, not in the kibbutz. Showed me the small room I could live in. Army barracks look better. Lavatory outside, also a sort of shower with a 12th century contraption to heat the water. I told Sally *why not* she said, despite all the primitive living conditions. I did not try to describe things better than they were. Sally accepted a job in the laundry room. Hanging laundry, folding laundry, pressing laundry. Sally found a good friend. The dentist clinic was run by a charming lady, Malvina, from the Argentine. Was there with a seven year old son. Sally altogether became very popular. Not me. When not at work, I was reading, even whilst eating or walking. One thing the kibbutzniks liked about me, I willingly gave them lifts to Tel-Aviv.

A very good sewing specialist ran the factory. Excellent to advise the girls how to work, no idea how to run a factory. No wonder they were losing money. I had never run a factory before. In Jerusalem I did not interfere with the actual production process. So I sat and observed how the factory is being run. I did so for a fortnight. Then, within a short time I doubled production. I was no genius. The previous system was just that bad. One of the Kibbutz members, Shmuel, was always by my side, a lady Kibbutz member I took as quality controller. Those were the only ones connected with the factory, apart from Yoel, the financial manager.

One thing was crystal clear. For Army work the factory was too small. For such cheap items one needs many more specialized machines, a bigger work force, a bigger place. To produce more expensive garments was the answer. The first and easiest to approach, someone I knew. Mr Gottlieb, owner of Gottex. He agreed to let us make bikinis. With our works manager, I visited a factory in Tel-Aviv producing these bikinis. Better learn from someone experienced than  learn by trial and error. Copy an already run-in outfit. Not just how to divide the operations. The cost of each operation and expected output. The Tel-Aviv workshop used the piece work system and so did we.

The first hitch, right from the beginning. The best girls earned just one third of what they did before. They just didn't produce enough. Soon we discovered why. Just a few days later the girls did not turn up in the morning at the usual hour. A couple of hours later they appeared together with the all mighty Trade Union officials. Here we are again ! This time it had nothing to do with being organized, wanted that we increase the piecework prices by a mere 300%. It would have simply meant not to accept the work from Gottex. Yoel, the kibbutz's financial manager arrived. He knew the calculation. The horse-trading started. I did not participate. Let the Mapainiks fight each other. Yoel whispered in my ear, *what increase can we agree to*. I whispered back, *the smallest increase and I leave*. Yoel *If you leave we close down. That exactly is what you should tell them*. My Kibbutz socialist won. Within a few weeks the girls earned more than double of what they had earned before. The girls revealed later, the Trade Unionists asked them to go slow, so they could fight out for better terms.

Life was quite different now. An excellent rest from the turbulent days in Jerusalem. Very few relations or friends came to visit us. By chance I discovered that many members of the nearby Kibbutz Kfar Ruppin came from Teplice. All of them I knew. Visited them a number of times.

An unusual visitor came in a limousine. Paul Kollek, a brother or cousin of Teddy Kollek. Henry, my brother wanted to know what happened that I am in a Kibbutz. He had a spinning mill in Caracas, Venezuela. Not having the time to come, asked Mr. Kollek to do it for him. *Must be expensive by taxi from Tel-Aviv and back* I said. *Not expensive, your brother pays*.

Again two visitors, I had never seen before, waited for me, as I returned from the factory. Israeli Intelligence. Wanted me to contact them next time I'll be in Tel-Aviv. The following week I gave them a ring. They came to take me to a villa on Sokolov street in Holon. This is six years after I came to Israel ! That they didn't believe me and kept an eye on me, I had suspected. My suspicion was confirmed by Sally's younger brother Aby, an officer in the Navy. Before I married Sally, he was questioned by them. Asked him if he knew who his sister is marrying and what he knew about me. They also spoke to the Kibbutz people, if they knew who I am.

They interrogated me for hours. In the end, *would I agree to be tested by a Lie-Detector ?* I had no objection. They will ring me to say when. Lucky I was working for a Mapai outfit. Yoel told them off good and proper. They never called me again, never came. (My cousin BenAmi introduced me some time ago to Mr Meridor, who he knew from his Etzel days. Meridor told me: *without a Mapai partner you won't succeed.*)

Working hours in the factory 5am to 2pm because of the extreme heat in that area. No air-conditioning. Our hut in the kibbutz had water dripping from the roof along creeping plants. That was the cooling system. I took the morning shower, before going to work, with cold water. It would take too long to heat the water with, what must have been a modern contraption in biblical times. All our meals in the dining room. No butter, only margarine. Sally and I preferred dry bread.

October 30, Sally gave birth to Nurit at the Afula hospital.

Nurit joined other babies in the Kibbutz nursery. A pram I had sent from England. There wasn't a decent pram to be had in Israel. The principal of Socialist society was understood, all should be poor. My cousin Hanna, grew up in our house, voted at the kibbutz for members not to have radios. It's a bourgeois contraption. We sent her a radio from England. That made it kosher.

Neve Eitan was getting really modern. An air-condition unit was installed in the babies room. The first one in the Kibbutz. Not every-one accepted this innovation. *It's not good for the babies.* One switched it on, the other turned it off. On-off all the time.

The year I promised to help run-in the factory was about to end in three months. Big textile outfits were built in the area. I visited them all. They have heard about me. Most interesting, my English and German. They were export orientated. I investigated if I can get a subsidized apartment in Beit Shean. It took a week, I got the permit. A two bedroom flat for $ 2,000. I didn't have the money. We decided to return to Tel-Aviv.

Sally actually liked the life in Neve Eitan. It gave her pleasure to be useful. They all liked her. She helped children with their English. It wasn't a huge enterprise of thousands of people. Just 120 members.

After 2pm, when the workers left, the work manager, Shmuel and myself checked the total produced of each operation. Made changes where necessary to avoid bottle necks in any of the operations. Arriving at the kibbutz one day, Shmuel's wife gave him a dressing-down, loud enough for many neighbours to hear. *Why don't you come back with every one, do you get more money, more food, do your children get a better education etc. etc?* In a nutshell she described socialist economy. **Performance adjusts itself to the least efficient.**

Beth Shean was known in biblical times as Scythopolis. Has a well preserved Roman amphitheatre. Excavations found temples from the middle and late Bronze Ages. Nearby a small lake, we used to swim in or just picnic nearby.

The Kibbutz was near the Jordan river, must see it! Expecting a real river, I was disappointed to see just a small rivulet. It's different during the rainy season. Turns into a wild stream, popular for rafting.

With the year up, we went first to Sally's parents small apartment till we rented one in north Tel-Aviv. From all the offers as a new immigrant I chose a detached house in Ramat Hasharon for 2,000 dollars. For Sally this was too far away. Sally was used to town living. We bought a two bedroom apartment in Ramat Gan for more than 30,000 dollars. Got a convenient mortgage through the British Immigration organization. Another mortgage Sally's uncle Fred Somekh arranged and guaranteed. Fred was head of the number one Israel's auditors, Somekh Chaikin. His son Gadi runs it now as an out of proportion larger concern.

I was offered jobs by sewing machine importers, who knew me from the time I bought from them. Chose to work for one. I refused a salary, on a commission basis only.

A government set-up of four people, representing the ministry of Trade and Industry, the ministry of Labour, the Trade Union and a Government industrial building outfit. The Head of the last    one was the proud father of the first and very pretty TV announcer Dalia Mazor. Never mind who these people represented, this was a group of very intelligent and very pleasant people to be with. They took me as the technical adviser. I travelled with them all over the country to see existing clothing and knitting workshops in development areas also discussing with the local authorities to set up new ones. This group knew how to provide industrial buildings, arrange funds for training labour and running-in costs, preferential loans for equipment.

The group meant well and I was in an advantageous position to sell equipment. I learned a new lesson. Government subsidized enterprises have very little chance to succeed. First of all the Trade Union interfered in everything. Their job, for the workers to get a maximum wage for minimum effort. They set unrealistically low production norms, which artificially increase the price of the product.

In big enterprises the Histadrut put their own people. It was very popular to push high ranking retired officers to leading positions. They had no idea how to run a factory. In development areas, the emphasis was to build clothing factories, as these are labour intensive. The stupid laws were such as to attract known crooks. They came to profit on the big moneys the government dished out. When they squeezed out all Government subsidies and loans, they disappeared. One, for these crooks most advantageous law, only new machinery was permitted to be imported. They brought newly painted old equipment with fictitious very high invoices. The government subsidy on the machinery was thus much higher than the actual cost. The so-called investor pocketed the difference. For this quasi industry to exist at all, high import duties protected them. Socialist wisdom at its best.

When a serious Swiss investor built a shirt factory in Beit Shemesh for 200 workers, he soon found out the system is foul. He just left. A local manufacturer took over without paying for it. The idea for the 200 workers not to lose their jobs. He squeezed out the maximum subsidies and left the country.

As one of my clients wanted only Husquarna sewing machines, I came to know Yigal Kimchi, who represented this Swedish factory. He had a huge shop in Herzl street, stretching from Achad Haam to nearly Rothschild and on two floors. His father-in-law had set up this *Palestine Orient Company*. He also represented Underwood typewriters and Columbia and His Master's Voice gramophone records. Yigal was Weitzman's, first Israeli president's secretary. His organization very small, but efficient. One very good secretary and two excellent mechanics. Our arrangement, I have one year to decide to become partner. I now sold all sewing machines and allied equipment through his company. These became, by turnover, by far the biggest part of the business.

A number of companies came, wanting for us, to market their products. The most interesting, a South African group, agents of *Brother*. Their idea, to import hand-knitting machines on a large scale. I loved the idea. I liked the people proposing it. Near to strike a deal, a young man enchanted Yigal with the idea of marketing Italian typewriters. No-one could convince Yigal that these were castles in the air. His wife came crying to me *you are the only one he will listen to*. He didn't. The two mechanics tried. No-one could. This young man gave figures of an expected huge turnover. To cope with it, needed two more secretaries, another four mechanics, keep a large stock. My opinion; he received a handsome money reward from the previous agent of that typewriter company from the high price Yigal paid.

I was not ready to witness the downfall of a good business and left. Yigal gave me the agency of Husquarna. As we all expected, the turnover with those new typewriters was less than half of the overheads. Within a few months the company closed down. The sad end of the Palestinian Orient Company.

I continued the business by myself but didn't like it. I decided on accessories. I wanted items that are in constant demand. Contacted a number of European companies. Import was the answer. I fought very tough odds. Marketing was easy, to cope with, the stupid bureaucratic restrictions, much more difficult. The least duty on my items was 80%, payable in cash only. The law did not allow suppliers' credit. Clearing goods, one had to show that goods are fully paid up. The reason given, *for the good name of Israel.* That this was a lie, probably the most stupid administers knew. Suppliers know how to protect themselves. They know how not to supply questionable clients.

Then came the Yom Kippur war. Not the political leaders, not the Generals saved Israel from certain defeat. The common people, the heroic soldiers did it. Despite heavy losses, they fought and held till a defence and then attack could be organized. That war finally showed the general public - the system is foul.

In the next elections, the Socialists lost control. The country could now grow. Israel had to export. Trade agreements were a must. The high protective duties fell. This increased import, thus competition with the local industry. The inefficient had to go. This effected Government, Trade Union and most of the Kibbutz concerns. Private enterprise became king. Gone was Golda Meir's dream:

Socialism in our generation.

Without natural resources,    Israel  grew  to  a  highly industrial powerhouse, out of all proportion to its size and population, despite the stupid administrative obstacles, many of which still exist.

# Chapter 17: Reminiscence

Our family had the luck to escape the horrors of Nazi Europe. Split in three groups we all managed to be together again in the middle of the war, after more than four years. As for myself, my parents' decision to send me to a Czech highschool was an important change in my life. I took to Czech mentality like a fish to water. Though the language barrier gave me difficulties at first. I overcame it very quickly. Then in Prague, after we had to leave our home in Teplice, for Henry and me to study at an all English school, parents' very good foresight. Our successful escape over the border to Poland. My successful five days' track to Warsaw when war broke out.

Our luck to survive the hell of Warsaw. The preferential treatment from the representatives of the Wehrmacht. Probably most important for us to succeed to reach the Russian border was the Oberleutnant, who gave us a lift in his jeep. Yet the confidence that we can do it gave us the German soldier from Karlsbad.

Same luck on the Russian side. The useful banker in Byalostock. The Jewish Joint providing us with a home in Wilno. The able forger of Czech official stamps. The Japanese consul Sugihara, The British consul in Kobe and the Quaker minister. The Quakers in Shanghai who looked after mother for a whole year. The Czech Military Mission in Shanghai who provided Henry and me with free transportation to England. The Red Cross in Shanghai, who let mother leave Japanese occupied territory. I survived 49 missions (600 operational hours) and a crash landing.

These were seven tough years. I started as a boy and grew to be a young man. Three times I was too weak to hold back my tears.

When on September 4, 1939, fourth day of the war, emotionally and physically exhausted, without food or drink, in the middle of nowhere, I saw no hope to ever reach Warsaw and see my mother and my brother again.

During mother's and Henry's emotional welcome two days later.

The day WW2 ended. I had survived.

Back in Czechoslovakia, my rapid advance in the Air Force and in the communist hierarchy. My foresight to get out of Czechoslovakia in time. The swiftness in my business success.

Having to leave England, not all was lost. I came to Israel at a good time to buy the most valuable real estate at ridiculously low prices.

I expected Henry to come to England, when I was arrested. Henry was the only one I could really trust. He could have easily turned the over a million dollar liquid assets into cash and liquidate the London business already then. I already suspected then that Steffi , encouraged by her not so honest husband will make father give her everything. Father looked after Steffi for 4 years. She was his baby.

Had Henry gone to England after father passed away, even then there must have still been enough assets to justify a few weeks' visit. I asked him that question. He didn't think it was that urgent, for a few days delay to make all the difference.

Yet, as Sally predicted from nothing I climbed up very fast. I learned to live with the system.

It was painful to see Czechoslovakia become a Russian satellite. Independent, democratic Czechoslovakia would have been my home. No *Numerus Clausus* for Jews in any of the Universities, no clubs closed to Jews, no questionnaires asking for race. We, who fought in WW2 were treated like heroes. In Israel I was a private. My war service sneered at as of no consequence.

In Czechoslovakia I was at home. Knew everybody. Had many friends. Had contact with people at the highest level. The social life on a very high standard. A real sacrifice to leave all this. Yet a Russian type country? Not again! I believed the Russian hijacking of the Czechoslovak leadership will not last long and I'll be back.

Cestomir Jeřábek started writing his diary in February 1948, expecting interesting developments. He, too expected the changes to be temporary. 10 years later he gave up.

Very difficult for me to understand the Slánsky affair.

*Rajcín,* head of military intelligence, deputy Minister of Defence.

*Závodsky.* Head of security in the Communist party. He fought in Spain. He knew how the Russians mistreated their Spanish fighters.

*Bedřich Geminder*, the top theoretician ?

*Andre Simon*, chief editor of the Communist Rudé Právo?

*Bedřich Hájek? Taussigová?* And others.

All in the centre of everything and not an inkling, no suspicion?

During my Prague visit in the winter of 1948, I planned one very important visit; to see Lada Novak. I had planned to go to Brno, where he was stationed, after my ski outing. All the years I regretted not to have gone to see him first

April 1990, my first Prague visit with Sally after the fall of the Soviet Empire, we went to Modřany, Lada's home town. At the municipality they tried for hours to trace him. Sometime later, through Air Force headquarters I was told Lada passed away in 1976. I Never got to know if he ever married, had children. As all airmen from the west, he was jailed. A communist since his childhood!

**The most fateful period for mother, Henry and me were the six weeks, from September 1 1939, when the war broke out till October 14, when we arrived in Russian occupied Wilno.**

# Chapter 18: World War    Two

No doubt Chamberlain and his Government were the leaders of appeasement from the minute Hitler came to power. The preceding political unrest they were not concerned with. Britain, France and the USA could have helped by cancelling the heavy war reparations forced on Germany. Even help financially with reconstruction. Return the stolen colonies. Yes, even re-negotiate the European territories taken from Germany in a pragmatic and reasonable way. Everything, to avoid Europe becoming a new battle field. This would have defeated the German revanchists in one stroke.

Even the Soviet Union could have been brought into the negotiations instead of fighting them. As a sign of good will, force Poland to accept the Curzon line, as the West actually suggested and the Poles ignored.

Transylvania could have been divided with more logic and Czechoslovakia made use the Swiss Canton system as intended.

Yet the culprit was Britain. Already the world's biggest Imperial Power, only interested to grab more, with eyes closed to the consequences.

In the end their protégé Hitler, did not keep his word, though this murderous outcast was for Chamberlain the perfect gentleman.

Persecution of Jews from   day one as Hitler came to power. A lot of sympathy, no deeds. Only Japan and the Philippines ready to receive unlimited numbers of Jews. This we didn't know nor care. Nothing much changed. German Jewish boys and girls kept on coming to our side of the border to participate in Maccabi competitions as carefree as before.

After the Evian conference, July 1938, we were no longer so confident. A Roosevelt instigated conference forced by public opinion to help the German and Austrian Jews. Only talk. Result zero. And in our area, considerable tension as the Nazis demanded the Sudetenland. Soon we were to find out the world is closing its gates to Jews.

There still was Palestine. The complicated system of certificates would surely be relaxed and this was the one country Jews could go to. Came the **White Paper.** The Balfour Declaration was part of Britain's Mandate over Palestine. But Britain was powerful, could ignore international obligations. Set Hitler a good example. Not enough that England split Palestine into two parts. One part for Arabs only. Now the western part to have an Arab majority. This meant more restrictions to Jewish immigration. **15,000 Jews to be admitted yearly for the next five years. From 1944 only with Arab consent.** Meaning zero. Thus the White Paper was a clear **declaration of war** against the Jewish Yishuv.

Ben Gurion: *We shall fight the White paper as though there is no war and fight the war as though there is no White Paper.* Well said. Yet Ben Gurion with the Jewish Agency were and remained subservient to Britain and fought against those Jews who took Ben Gurion's words seriously. **In this respect the Jewish Agency was for Britain, what the Judenrat was for Germany.**

To make sure Churchill does not forget; the **Middle Eastern War Council** not only reminded Churchill but also **recommended** *a firm reassertion of the White Paper policy of 1939,* **which gives the Arabs the right to stop Jewish immigration after the end of March 1944.** ( Lord Cherwell. Martin Gilbert: Auschwitz and the Allies. Page 147)

During my months at Jerusalem's Orgil hotel, I heard about the Jewish struggle for independence from Menahem Begin. I knew very little about Etzel and Lehi. I followed their struggle only after the war. It was clear England had no intention to give up Palestine peacefully. Not to the Jews anyway. England was, as Begin declared in 1942, number one enemy of the Jews.

Being free in a democratic country during the war, I believed to be well informed about events on the Continent. After I met survivors from concentration camps, I realized the media was not so free. We did not know what was really happening. All through the war we believed the media that all people under German occupation suffered equally. Never an inkling, a hint that the Nazis singled out the Jews for annihilation.

It is heart breaking to read how many opportunities to save Jews were missed. Only that they were not really missed. **It was Allied policy <u>not</u> to help the Jews.** Britain even **refused** to broadcast to Europe what deportation really meant and not to trust the Judenrat. Informed by the very efficient scientists of Bletchley Park, Churchill knew about Nazi atrocities since 1941. The Nazis themselves were so determined to preserve the secrecy of their program of mass extermination, precisely because they feared that release of such information would interfere with their plan. The BBC helped them to keep that secret.

The only ones in a position to stop the rule of the most bloodthirsty and criminal regime in human history from the inside, were the German Generals. If they enjoyed their spectacular victories in 1939/40, they did not want to fight Russia. They knew their army did not have the power to fight on two fronts. Hitler told them the war is to forestall an imminent Russian attack. In the first days of Barbarossa the Generals knew it was a lie. Worse. Within the first weeks the German Generals also understood they cannot win the war. We only heard of the rapid advance, not at what price.

*The opening battle in June 1941 revealed to us for the first time the new Soviet Army. Our casualties were up to fifty percent.*(General Blumentritt to Liddell Hart, page 225).

The Germans also discovered the Russians had better equipment. *Their equipment was very good even in 1941, especially the tanks. Their artillery was excellent, and also most of the infantry weapons-their rifles were more modern than ours and had a more rapid rate of fire. Their T34 tank was the finest in the world.* (General Kleist to Liddell Hart, page 221)

The Russian war production outstripped the German by far. General Halder (Chief of the General Staff) told Hitler, *Intelligence had information that 600 to 700 tanks a month were coming out of the Russian factories in the Ural Mountains and elsewhere.* ( Liddell Hart, page 195}

*German production was 85 tanks a month* (Generaloberst Erhard Rauss, Fighting in Hell, page 203)

It was not too late to stop that war. *Even before the final assault on Moscow (October 1941) Generals von Rundstedt and von Leeb urged that the German Army should withdraw to their original front in Poland.* (Liddell Hart- the German Generals talk, page 194).

In contrast the Goebbels disinformation apparatus announced that same October:

*The Russian Moloch already lies prostrate and will not rise again.* ("Stalingrad" by Heinz Schröter, war correspondent's staff, Sixth Army)

The German Generals were cowards. They did not act They could have saved some of the honour for Germany. Instead they let Hitler kill one General after another. Helped sacrifice their own German youth for his adventures. Let Hitler make the Germans the most brutal nation in history.

We criticized the Allied leaders' war conduct during a public debate in the Bahamas, which nearly got me into trouble. From preventing victory in Libya in 1940 to the failure to end the war in 1942.

*Roosevelt told Churchill April, 1942, he is sending Lloyd Hopkins and General Marshall with a plan for a Second front in Europe, in France, a plan which I hope will be received with enthusiasm by Russia* (2194 days of war. Page 223)

The British public was crying out for a **SECOND FRONT** in Europe already in 1941 when the Germans attacked Russia. If there were excuses then, there were none in 1942. There was no Western Wall. The Wehrmacht in the West depleted. The Allies had complete Air supremacy. The whole of the German army thousands of miles away in Russia. The German Generals said within hours the Allies could have reached the heart of Germany.

Millions of German soldiers would have been cut off from supplies. Millions of Germans in East Prussia and occupied territories as well.

Yes, a Second Front in Europe in 1942, the result an unimaginable catastrophe for the Germans. A catastrophe the Germans deserved. The Germans loved this painter murderer from Austria. He could stand unprotected in a car. *Ein Reich, ein Volk ein Führer* they chanted. Women were still screaming *Sieg Heil*, whilst their husbands and sons were starving, freezing, bleeding in faraway Russia. Still, more Germans would stay alive, had the war not dragged on another three years.

The German Generals refused to start the spring offensive in 1942. Other Generals took over. But why again just refuse, why not kill Hitler and his murderous lot. Free the concentration camps and the slave labourers. Save some dignity for the German people. What could they achieve by nearly three years of retreat ? Only death to their own people at home and at the front.

General Heinrici, wrote home on August 1, 1941, *Der Krieg hier kommt uns sehr teuer. Ob er wirklich nötig war ?* Yet he lead the defense of Berlin. Did he plan to defeat the Red Army in front of Berlin ? For Hitler there was nothing left but suicide. He wanted for the whole

German nation to go with him. Only in the very last moment did the Germans disobey and not destroy their industries. The U-boat commanders ignored the order to commit suicide by ramming Allied ships. Too late. The total guilt weighs heavily on the German nation.

**TORCH**, the Allied landing in North Africa in November 1942 was for us and the people in England a terrible shock. Couldn't see a smile on anyone's face. One thing was clear, Churchill and Roosevelt were in no hurry to end the war. Even 1943 was too early for them

**Let Hitler solve the Jewish problem for them.**

If this was not clear enough to understand, came the top secret Bermuda conference to confirm it.

The other reason to prolong the war.

**To cause more losses to the Russians.**

*This is the seed of the cold war instead of peaceful co-existence that we all wished and deserved.*

Four months later the Allies landed at the most southerly tip of Italy. Let the Italians, too, taste Nazi rule ! If our great war leaders didn't lift a finger to help the Jews, they now helped Hitler to get hold of another **43,000 Jews of Italy whom Mussolini had protected from deportation, also many thousand more Jews who lived, or had found refuge, in the Italian occupied zones of France and Croatia, along the Dalmatian**

**coast, in Albania, in Greece, Corfu, the island of Rhodes.** (Martin Gilbert, Auschwitz and the Allies, page 152)

**Many more millions of soldiers and civilians of all nations sacrificed for dragging on the war for another three years is on the conscience of the Allied leaders.**

Allies could have freed all of Europe before the Russians. There would be no Yalta sell-out. Czechoslovakia would not have to suffer another forty years under Russian oppression. And Věra, the girl I so much loved since age 11, would be alive. She was taken to Auschwitz September 6, 1943. Age 19.

In 1942 the Allies would have been partners in victory. The Russians too weak to make demands. When at last the Allies did land in France, June 1944, Russia had already won the war. They now dictated the terms.

It is time to open all WW2 files. Hopefully the most damaging orders and decision were not shredded at the time. It would be interesting to read Churchill's three hours speech on October 5, 1943, in which he said:

*We mustn't weaken Germany too much, we may need her against Russia.* (Oliver Harvey's diary, page 304)

## Chapter 19: End of Diary

Henry passed away in 1994.

My very numerous travels with Sally came to an end, when after returning from Europe at the end of 2002, Sally fell ill. She passed away in 2006.

A year later I went with Nurit, Boaz and Guy to Prague to meet most of Henry's children and grand-children from England. We also visited Teplice, for them to see where we grew up. We were met by Dr. Drbohlav, professor from Duchcov, Pavel Koukal, writer, his wife Věra, poet, (grand-daughter of the director of the Duchcov high school, where I studied). For lunch we were joined by a classmate of mine, Libuše Rídelová. She has the highest Czech award for theatre actors.

I got in touch with Dr Drbohlav and Pavel Koukal as a result of a newspaper advert they placed with my pre-war photo. They had decided to find out the fate of Jews who had studied at the Duchcov Reálné Gymnasium.

They also organized for Duchcov to have a memorial statue for Jews, who perished in the holocaust.

The super remark came from Charles, one of Henry's grandchildren. Susie's son.

*WHY DID YOU LEAVE SUCH A LOVELY PLACE*

1931 – With his brother Henry and sister Steffi

1938 At home in Teplice

Parents 1935

Henry 1938

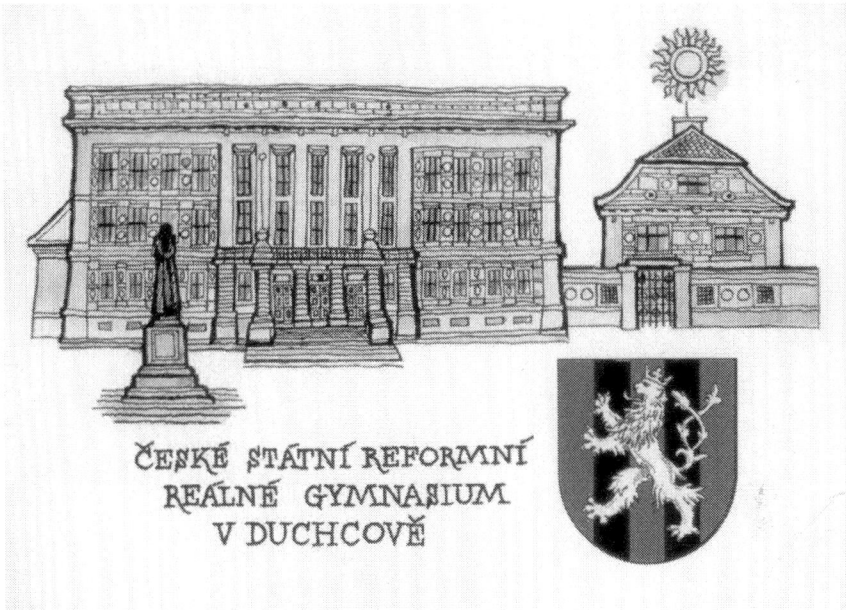

ČEŠKÉ ŠTÁTNÍ REFORMNÍ
REALNÉ GYMNAŠIUM
V DUCHCOVĚ

First year High School – Peter in last row, extreme right. One of three Jews in class.
Lustigova and Lebochovic perished in the holocaust.

Bernhard Apfelbaum und Frau

erlauben sich die

בר מצוה (Konfirmation)

ihres Sohnes Salo, welche am Samstag, 5. Jänner 1935
im großen Tempel zu Teplitz-Schönau statt-
findet, höflichst anzuzeigen

Teplitz-Schönau, (Meczerystraße 1543) im Jänner 1935

With Henry and English soldier 1941. Singapore

With mother in Kaunas 1940

With the second crew – 311 squadron - 1944

With first crew before the crash landing

Henry – RAF mechanic

Lada Novak

In Czech uniform - 1945

B – 24 Liberator

Věra Müllerová

Orlon coats I supplied from Israel

MUSEUM 7158

*Peter Arton*

55, Portland Place,
London, W.1

---

Telephone:
METropolitan 8771-2-3

Cable:
Limicloth, London

# H. & B. CLOTHIERS, LTD.

MANUFACTURERS,

**Exporters and Importers**

31, FINSBURY SQUARE,
LONDON, E.C.2

Represented by

# Groom poses for wedding—then back to jail

THE WEDDING GROUP: Peter Arton, who left jail for the party, with his bride-to-be yesterday. On his left are his parents. On her right is her mother.

## Watched by detective

By MICHAEL FITZGERALD

CHAMPAGNE glasses clinked, the bridal couple smiled—and then Prague-and Peter Arton made out of the happy flat and went back to his cell in Brixton Prison.

It was yesterday's pre-wedding party with a difference.

Today Arton will marry attractive Claudia Michaelis, aged 24, at St John's Wood, at a Marylebone Register Office.

Afterwards, with a Scotland Yard escort at his side, he and his bride will drive to London Airport, and be put aboard a plane for Israel.

### CLOSED TO HIM

All Britain, the country to which he came as a child refugee from Czechoslovakia and where he fought in the World of Britain as a R.A.F. pilot, will be closed to him.

Security men arrested him on Thursday in the park of the wedding at Hampstead Synagogue.

His imprisonment and deportation follow a week-long order to security men into details about Czechs in

London being passed to Communist embassies here.

He was allowed out of Brixton for nine hours yesterday under a gentleman's agreement to say nothing.

With a detective by his side, he drove to his parents' flat—a week had in Portland-place to changing into the wedding suit bespoke for the signature wedding, and went to marry Miss Michaelis's flat in St John's Wood.

His father, Mr Ben Arton, a prosperous textile merchant, who had a heart attack when his son was arrested, was too ill. So did a detective.

### CHAMPAGNE

The day was gay with flowers. Arton and Miss Michaelis laughed and sipped champagne. All the guests wore the clothes they would have worn at the synagogue wedding.

But there were no speeches at the party, no member of either's family. And through the speeches, no unobtrusive guard of security.

As he posed with his bride-to-be for the wedding picture, the small family circle rallied round.

Then the party ended—"I must go back to jail as usual," said Arton.

THEY SMILED—and nobody spoke of to-day's parting, when Peter and Claudia will leave their families.

They smiled as they posed for this wedding preview picture. But there was sadness, too.

## MYSTERY FIRES I

MYSTERY fires are devastating hundreds of acres of Ashdown Forest. Police and firemen believe

Wedding day 1960

Sally and sisters and brothers - 1997

Sally at a casino in Toronto

Sally with Eva and her husband in Prague

With PhD. Drbohlav

With the Bogners

Printed in Great Britain
by Amazon